FRENCH LISTENING WORKBOOK

50 French Listening Activities for Daily Practice

DYLANE MOREAU

TABLE OF CONTENTS

PREFACE

Welcome to the *French Listening Workbook*, a unique resource designed to help you improve your French listening skills. This workbook offers a collection of 50 chapters, each featuring daily activities that focus on essential aspects of the French language, including specific sounds, silent letters, liaisons, and more. By honing these critical listening elements, you'll gain confidence in understanding spoken French in everyday situations.

The activities in this workbook are made into bite-size lessons, allowing you to practice French daily even when you have little time for your learning journey.

The varied and interactive exercises encourage you to engage deeply with the material. You'll work through activities such as filling in missing words, putting the text back in the correct order, identifying silent letters, and spotting liaisons in sentences. These exercises are designed to sharpen your ear for the nuances of French pronunciation and improve your overall comprehension.

To support your learning, free downloadable audio accompanies each chapter, allowing you to practice your listening skills in real-time. Whether studying independently or supplementing classroom learning, this workbook provides practical tools to help you improve steadily.

The *French Listening Workbook* is part of a broader series that also includes the *French Vocabulary Workbook* and the *French Grammar Workbook*. Together, they give you a complete set of resources to strengthen your French in all areas.

I hope this workbook becomes a valuable tool in mastering French listening.

Happy listening!

Dylane

HOW TO USE THIS BOOK

This book is designed to improve your French listening skills with 50 listening activities. To maximize your learning experience, here are some helpful tips:

- Take advantage of the note pages throughout the book. Keep track of the vocabulary you learned, the questions you got right and the ones you got wrong, as well as the words you struggle to hear. Come back to your notes often to review them.
- Pace Yourself: Instead of doing all the lessons and exercises in one sitting, try focusing on one chapter and one activity per day. Since this book includes 50 chapters, you will have 50 days of French listening practice.
- Do the exercises: Each chapter includes exercises to help you practice your listening. It can be a missing-word text or an exercise focused on specific sounds. Try to write down as much as possible when doing the activities. Make your listening count, but if your spelling isn't right, it's nothing to worry about.
- Improve Your Listening Skills: This book is obviously about listening, but take advantage of all the audio, including the recording of the vocabulary lists. Listen to the audio and read the text simultaneously to improve your French listening skills!

I think you are ready to improve your French listening skills!

Have fun learning!

HOW TO USE THE VOCABULARY LISTS

Each vocabulary list contains the relevant words for the topic and is presented following the lesson.

To optimize your learning experience, here are some important things to consider when using the vocabulary list:

- Whenever possible, all nouns are converted to their singular form so you can easily recognize their gender. Some nouns, such as profession, have masculine and feminine forms.
- All adjectives are presented in both masculine and feminine forms.
- Verbs are listed in their infinitive form to help you recognize their base form.
- Additionally, each vocabulary word is accompanied by its part of speech when possible, which is indicated in the legend below.

Legend

adj – adjective	**adjectif**
adv – adverb	**adverbe**
n – noun	**nom** (when both genders are given)
nf – feminine noun	**nom féminin**
nm – masculine noun	**nom masculin**
prép – preposition	**préposition**
pp – past participle	**participe présent**
v – verb	**verbe**

HOW TO DOWNLOAD THE AUDIO

To download the audio files of all the recordings of this book, visit

www.theperfectfrench.com/french-listening-workbook-audios

or scan the **QR code** below.

After entering your email, the link for the audio download will be sent directly to your inbox with step-by-step instructions. If you encounter an issue, please send me an email at **info@theperfectfrench.com**

MES AMIS VIENNENT DÎNER

MY FRIENDS ARE COMING FOR DINNER

1

AUDIO 1.1 ◀))

1. Écoutez l'audio et **lisez l'histoire** en même temps.
Listen to the audio and read the story at the same time.

Mes amis viennent dîner

Ce soir, mes amis viennent dîner chez moi. On est quatre en tout. Une fois par mois, un de nous reçoit les autres pour un repas simple. C'est une bonne façon de passer du temps ensemble. Ce n'est pas beaucoup de travail vu que c'est une fois tous les quatre mois. Cette fois-ci, je prépare une lasagne avec les tomates de mon jardin. J'ai aussi fait du pain ce matin pour faire du pain à l'ail. Il est déjà prêt, je n'ai plus qu'à le mettre au four avant de servir. C'est la première fois que je fais une lasagne mais elle a l'air très bonne. Pour l'apéritif, j'ai prévu une bouteille de champagne et des amuse-bouches. En dessert, ça sera un bol de glace avec des fraises et des framboises. Même si on fait toujours un repas simple, cela prend quand même toute la journée à préparer. Il faut ranger, nettoyer, préparer le repas et mettre la table. Encore heureux qu'on est que quatre car dans mon petit appartement, j'ai seulement assez de place pour une table de quatre personnes. Mes amis arriveront dans une heure donc je dois aller me préparer pour être à l'heure.

TRANSLATION

My Friends Are Coming for Dinner

This evening, my friends are coming to my house for dinner. There are four of us in total. Once a month, one of us hosts the others for a meal. It's a good way to spend time together. It's not a lot of work, considering it's once every four months. This time, I'm preparing a lasagna with tomatoes from my garden. I also made some bread this morning to make garlic bread. It's already ready; all I have to do is put it in the oven before serving. This is my first time making lasagna, but it looks really good. For the aperitif, I planned a bottle of champagne and appetizers. For dessert, it will be a bowl of ice cream with strawberries and raspberries. Even though we always make a simple meal, it still takes all day to prepare. You have to tidy up, clean, prepare the meal and set the table. I am glad that there are only four of us because, in my small apartment, I only have enough room for a four-person table. My friends will arrive in an hour, so I have to get ready to be on time.

2. **Écoutez l'audio 1.1** et ajoutez **les mots manquants**.
Listen to the audio 1.1 and add the missing words.

Mes amis viennent dîner

Ce soir, mes amis viennent dîner chez   . On est quatre en tout. Une

fois par mois, un de nous reçoit les autres pour un   simple. C'est

une bonne façon de passer du temps   . Ce n'est pas beaucoup de

           vu que c'est une fois tous les quatre mois. Cette fois-ci, je prépare une

lasagne avec les   de mon jardin. J'ai aussi fait du pain ce matin pour

faire du pain à l'ail. Il est déjà prêt, je n'ai plus qu'à le mettre au   avant

de servir. C'est la première fois que je fais une lasagne mais elle a l'air très bonne. Pour l'apéritif,

j'ai prévu une   de champagne et des amuse-bouches. En dessert, ça

sera un bol de glace avec des   et des framboises. Même si on fait

toujours un repas simple, cela prend quand même toute la journée à   .

Il faut ranger, nettoyer, préparer le repas et mettre la   . Encore heureux

qu'on est que quatre car dans mon petit   , j'ai seulement assez de place

pour une table de quatre personnes. Mes amis arriveront dans une

donc je dois aller me préparer pour être à l'heure.

AUDIO 1.2 ◄))

VOCABULARY

Le soir nm | *The evening*
Un ami – Une amie n | *A friend*
Un dîner nm | *A dinner*
Quatre | *Four*
Recevoir v | *To host*
Les autres nm | *The others*
Un repas simple nm + adj | *A simple meal*
Une façon nf | *A way*
Passer du temps | *To spend time*
Du travail nm | *Work*
Une fois nf | *Once*
Préparer v | *To prepare*
Une lasagne nf | *A lasagna*
Une tomate nf | *A tomato*

Le jardin nm | *The garden*
Du pain nm | *Bread*
Du pain à l'ail nm | *Garlic bread*
Prêt – Prête adj | *Ready*
Mettre au four v | *To put in the oven*
Servir v | *To serve*
Bon – Bonne adj | *Good*
Un apéritif nm | *Aperitif*
Une bouteille de champagne nf |
A bottle of champagne
Des amuse-bouches nm | *Appetizers*
Un dessert nm | *A dessert*
Un bol de glace nm | *A bowl of ice cream*
Une fraise nf | *A strawberry*

Une framboise nf | *A raspberry*
Prendre v | *To take*
Ranger v | *To tidy up*
Nettoyer v | *To clean*
Mettre la table v | *To set the table*
Un petit appartement adj + nm | *A small apartment*

De la place nf | *Room*
Une table nf | *A table*
Une personne nf | *A person*
Arriver v | *To arrive*
Se préparer v | *To get ready*

LE SON IN
THE SOUND IN

2

The sound **in** has nine possible spellings in French. They are all pronounced the same way. It's all about the spelling. Note that **un** and **um** have different pronunciations in southern France, but the sound is included if you are learning Parisian French.

AUDIO 2.1 ◀》

in	**Un lapin** nm | *A rabbit*
im before b and p	**Un timbre** nm | *A stamp*
ain	**Un pain** nm | *A loaf of bread*
aim	**La faim** nf | *Hunger*
ein	**La peinture** nf | *Paint*
yn	**Un lynx** nm | *A lynx*
ym	**Un tympan** nm | *An eardrum*
un	**Lundi** nm | *Monday*
um	**Un parfum** nm | *A perfume*

This exercise, "Listen and repeat," is divided into four different parts:

1. The sound only
2. The sound in syllables
3. The sound in words
4. Write down the words you hear

AUDIO 2.2 ◀》

1. Écoutez **le son in** et répétez après moi.
   *Listen to the sound **in** and repeat after me.*

in – im – ain – aim – ein – yn – ym – un – um

AUDIO 2.3 ◀》

2. Écoutez **le son in** dans **les différentes syllabes** et répétez après moi.
   *Listen to the sound **in** in the different syllables and repeat after me.*

bin – cin – din – fin – jin – lin – min – nin – pin – rin – sin – tin – vin – zin

3. Écoutez **les différents mots** incluant le son **in** et répétez après moi.
   *Listen to the different words including the sound **in** and repeat after me.*

Un b<u>ain</u>	Loint<u>ain</u>
Chac<u>un</u>	M<u>ain</u>tenant
Cr<u>ain</u>dre	Un p<u>ein</u>tre
Ét<u>ein</u>dre	Un sap<u>in</u>
H<u>um</u>ble	Un tr<u>ain</u>

4. Écrivez **les mots** que vous entendez. Si vous ne comprenez pas le mot complet, écrivez une ou deux syllabes.
   Write down the words you hear. If you don't understand the full word, write one or two syllables.

1.	11. Un
2.	12. Un
3. Un	13. Une
4. Un	14. Un
5. Un	15.
6. Un	16. Un
7. La	17.
8. Un	18.
9. Un	19. Du
10.	20. Un

VOCABULARY

Atteindre v | *To reach*	**Un copain** nm | *A friend*
Un bain nm | *A bath*	**Un coussin** nm | *A pillow*
Brun adj | *Brown*	**Craindre** v | *To fear*
Chacun adj | *Each*	**Un dessin** nm | *A drawing*
Un cintre nm | *A hanger*	**Éteindre** v | *To turn off*

La fin nf | *The end*
Un frein nm | *A brake*
Un grain nm | *A grain*
Humble adj | *Humble*
Impossible adj | *Impossible*
Un jardin nm | *A garden*
Lointain adj | *Distant*
Un magasin nm | *A store*
Une main nf | *A hand*
Maintenant adv | *Now*
Un matin nm | *A morning*

Un peintre nm | *A painter*
Plein adj | *Full*
Un poussin nm | *A chick*
Un sapin nm | *A pine tree*
Simple adj | *Simple*
Teindre v | *To dye*
Un train nm | *A train*
Du vin nm | *Wine*
Un voisin nm | *A neighbour*

LA TEMPÊTE DE NEIGE
THE SNOWSTORM

3

AUDIO 3.1 ◄))

1. Écoutez l'audio et **lisez l'histoire** en même temps.
Listen to the audio and read the story at the same time.

La tempête de neige

Tout est calme dans le petit village de Mégève. Il n'est que 18 heures mais les habitants sont déjà chez eux. Il n'y a personne dans les rues et pas de voiture sur la route. La météo prévoit une tempête de neige ce soir. Mégève est un village en montagne donc les habitants sont habitués aux tempêtes de neige. Apparemment, il va tomber plus d'un mètre de neige en quelques heures. C'est la première tempête de neige cette année. Les pelles à neige sont prêtes et les déneigeuses attendent impatiemment dans les garages. L'hiver peut maintenant commencer.

TRANSLATION

The Snowstorm

Everything is calm in the small village of Mégève. It's only 6 p.m., but the residents are already at home. There is no one in the streets and no cars on the road. The weather forecast is calling for a snowstorm this evening. Megève is a mountain village, so residents are used to snowstorms. Apparently, more than a meter of snow will fall in a few hours. This is the first snowstorm this year. The snow shovels are ready, and the snowplows are waiting impatiently in the garages. Winter can now begin.

2. Écoutez l'audio 3.1 et **numérotez les phrases de 1 à 9 pour les remettre dans l'ordre.**
Listen to the audio 3.1 and number the sentences from 1 to 9 to put them in order.

– C'est la première tempête de neige cette année.

– Il n'est que 18 heures mais les habitants sont déjà chez eux.

– L'hiver peut maintenant commencer.

– Il n'y a personne dans les rues et pas de voiture sur la route.

– Apparemment, il va tomber plus d'un mètre de neige en quelques heures.

– La météo prévoit une tempête de neige ce soir.

– Tout est calme dans le petit village de Mégève.

– Les pelles à neige sont prêtes et les déneigeuses attendent impatiemment dans les garages.

– Mégève est un village en montagne donc les habitants sont habitués aux tempêtes de neige.

AUDIO 3.2 ◀ꓵ))

VOCABULARY

Une tempête de neige nf | *A snowstorm*
Calme adj | *Calm*
Un petit village adj + nm | *A little village*
Un habitant – Une habitante n | *A resident*
Personne pr | *Nobody*
Une rue nf | *A street*
Une voiture nf | *A car*
La route nf | *The road*
La météo nf | *The weather forecast*
Prévoir v | *To call for*
Ce soir adv | *Tonight*
Une montagne nf | *A mountain*
Être habitué – habituée v | *To be used to*

Tomber v | *To fall*
Un mètre nm | *A metre*
La première | *The first*
Cette année nf | *This year*
Une pelle à neige nf | *A snow shovel*
Prêt – Prête adj | *Ready*
Une déneigeuse nf | *A snow plow*
Attendre v | *To wait*
Impatiemment adv | *Impatiently*
Un garage nm | *A garage*
L'hiver nm | *Winter*
Commencer v | *To start*

LE SON AN
THE SOUND AN

4

The sound **an** has five possible spellings in French. They are all pronounced the same way. It's all about the spelling. **Aon** is a specific spelling for **Un paon** – *A peacock*.

AUDIO 4.1 ◄))

an	**Un éléph<u>an</u>t** nm	*An elephant*
am before b and p	**Une l<u>am</u>pe** nf	*A lamp*
en	**Une t<u>en</u>te** nf	*A tent*
em before b and p	**R<u>em</u>bourser** v	*To reimburse*
aon	**Un p<u>aon</u>** nm	*A peacock*

This exercise, "Listen and repeat," is divided into four different parts:

1. The sound only
2. The sound in syllables
3. The sound in words
4. Write down the words you hear

AUDIO 4.2 ◄))

1. Écoutez **le son an** et répétez après moi.
   *Listen to the sound **an** and repeat after me.*

   an – am – en – am – aon

AUDIO 4.3 ◄))

2. Écoutez **le son an** dans **les différentes syllabes** et répétez après moi.
   *Listen to the sound **an** in the different syllables and repeat after me.*

   ban – can – dan – fan – jan – lan – man – nan – pan – ran – san – tan – van – zan

AUDIO 4.4 ◄))

3. Écoutez **les différents mots** incluant le son **an** et répétez après moi.
   *Listen to the different words including the sound **an** and repeat after me.*

Une <u>am</u>poule	Un diam<u>an</u>t
Une ch<u>an</u>ce	<u>En</u>semble

Import**ant**	Une pl**an**te
Mam**an**	Le t**em**ps
Nov**em**bre	Le v**en**tre

AUDIO 4.5 ◄》

4. Écrivez **les mots** que vous entendez. Si vous ne comprenez pas le mot complet, écrivez une ou deux syllabes.
Write down the words you hear. If you don't understand the full word, write one or two syllables.

1.	Une	11.	Une
2.		12.	Un
3.	Un	13.	
4.		14.	Un
5.		15.	Un
6.	Une	16.	
7.		17.	Le
8.	Un	18.	
9.	Un	19.	Un
10.		20.	Le

AUDIO 4.6 ◄》

VOCABULARY

Une ampoule nf | *A lightbulb*
Une banque nf | *A bank*
Blanc – Blanche adj | *White*
Un champion nm | *A champion*
Une chance nf | *A chance*
Décembre nm | *December*
Dedans adv | *Inside*
Une dent nf | *A tooth*
Un diamant nm | *A diamond*
Emporter v | *To take away*

Un enfant nm | *A child*
Ensemble adv | *Together*
Un fantôme nm | *A ghost*
Grand – Grande adj | *Big*
Important – Importante adj | *Important*
Une jambe nf | *A leg*
Un jambon nm | *Ham*
Maman nf | *Mom*
Manger v | *To eat*
Un manteau nm | *A coat*

Novembre nm | *November*
Un pantalon nm | *A pair of pants*
Penser v | *To think*
Une plante nf | *A plant*
Le printemps nm | *Spring*

Rentrer v | *To return*
Un serpent nm | *A snake*
Le temps nm | *The weather*
Le vent nm | *The wind*
Le ventre nm | *The belly*

QUEL MOT EST-CE QUE JE PRONONCE ?
WHAT WORD DO I PRONOUNCE?

AUDIO 5.1

Écoutez l'audio et entourez le mot que je prononce. Chaque mot est répété deux fois.
La liste des mots est traduite après cet exercice.
Listen to the audio and circle the word I say. Each word is repeated twice. The list of words is translated after this exercise.

1. Poisson – Poison	8. Chasse – Chasser	15. Visse – Fils
2. Bougie – Bouger	9. Livre – Libre	16. Gare – Guerre
3. Chaud – Chaude	10. Poule – Pôle	17. Cou – Coule
4. Cacher – Casser	11. Chapeau – Château	18. Carte – Quart
5. Port – Porte	12. Brun – Brune	19. Blanc – Blé
6. Plage – Page	13. Feu – Fou	20. Pont – Ponce
7. Chanter – Enchanté	14. Fille – File	

AUDIO 5.2

VOCABULARY

Un poisson nm | *A fish*
Du poison nm | *Poison*
Une bougie nf | *A candle*
Bouger v | *To move*
Chaud – Chaude adj | *Hot*
Cacher v | *To hide*
Casser v | *To break*
Un port nm | *A port*
Une porte nf | *A door*
La plage nf | *The beach*
Une page nf | *A page*
Chanter v | *To sing*
Enchanté – Enchantée adj | *Delighted*
La chasse nf | *Hunt*
Chasser v | *To hunt*
Un livre nm | *A book*
Libre adj | *Free*
Une poule nf | *A chicken*
Un pôle nm | *A pole*

Un chapeau nm | *A hat*
Un château nm | *A castle*
Brun – Brune adj | *Brown*
Du feu nm | *A fire*
Fou – Folle adj | *Crazy*
Une fille nf | *A daughter*
Une file nf | *A line*
Une visse nf | *A screw*
Un fils nm | *A son*
Une gare nf | *A train station*
Une guerre nf | *A war*
Le cou nm | *The neck*
Coule (Couler) v | *To flow*
Une carte nf | *A map*
Un quart nm | *A quarter*
Blanc – Blanche adj | *White*
Du blé nm | *Wheat*
Un pont nm | *A bridge*
Ponce (Poncer) v | *To sand*

LA LETTRE MUETTE E
THE SILENT LETTER E

6

What is a Silent Letter?

A silent letter in French is a letter that is not pronounced. A silent letter is usually at the end of a word.

The letter **e** is the most common silent letter in French. 99% of the time, if a word ends with **e**, it will be silent.

Here are the three types of words where you can find the silent letter **e** in French:

AUDIO 6.1 🔊

At the end of nouns, adjectives and pronouns
(not including short words of 2 or 3 letters: **je – de – le – me**)

Une balance nf | *A scale*
Une danse nf | *A dance*

Égoïste adj | *Selfish*
Malade adj | *Sick*

Elle pr | *She*

AUDIO 6.2 🔊

When a verb is conjugated with je – il – elle – on

Je parle v | *I am speaking*
Je garde v | *I am keeping*

Il parle v | *He is speaking*
Il chante v | *He is singing*

Elle parle v | *She is speaking*
Elle marche v | *She is walking*

On regarde v | *We are watching*
On discute v | *We are talking*

Note that e and s are silent when a noun, an adjective, a pronoun, or a conjugated verb ending with e is plural.

> **Je garde – Tu gardes** | *I am keeping – You are keeping*
> **Une danse – Des danses** | *A dance – Dances*
> **Elle – Elles** | *She – They*

1. Écoutez la différence lorsque **la lettre e** est **prononcée** et **non prononcée**.
   *Listen to the difference when the letter **e** is pronounced and not pronounced.*

Me | *Me*
Une larme | *A tear*

2. Écoutez ces 20 phrases et **entourez les mots** où **la lettre e est muette**.
   *Listen to these 20 sentences and circle the words where the letter **e** is silent.*

1. Elle veut prendre de meilleures habitudes.
2. L'herbe n'arrête pas de pousser ces dernières semaines !
3. Tu es encore jeune pour choisir.
4. Éteins la télévision si tu quittes la pièce.
5. Je ne pense pas qu'elle soit jalouse.
6. Ce pull est trop large pour moi.
7. Il est tout le temps malade.
8. Fais attention à la marche.
9. Rien de mieux qu'une balade dans la nature.
10. Je mange souvent une banane à 4 heures.
11. C'est nécessaire d'être bien préparé.
12. Il neige depuis ce matin.
13. On plante des carottes chaque année.
14. J'ai perdu la page de mon livre.
15. N'oublie pas ton écharpe.
16. Il y a toujours des travaux sur l'autoroute.
17. Est-ce que tu as le temps de prendre un café ?
18. J'aime bien le lait de soja mais je préfère le lait d'amandes.
19. C'est mon anniversaire dans une semaine.
20. On loue toujours une voiture quand on voyage.

TRANSLATION

1. *She wants to develop better habits.*
2. *The grass hasn't stopped growing these last few weeks!*
3. *You are still young to choose.*
4. *Turn off the television if you leave the room.*
5. *I don't think she's jealous.*
6. *This sweater is too big for me.*
7. *He is sick all the time.*
8. *Watch out for the step.*
9. *Nothing better than a walk in nature.*
10. *I often eat a banana at 4 o'clock.*
11. *It is necessary to be well prepared.*
12. *It's been snowing since this morning.*
13. *We plant carrots every year.*
14. *I lost the page of my book.*
15. *Don't forget your scarf.*
16. *There is always work on the highway.*
17. *Do you have time for coffee?*
18. *I like soy milk but prefer almond milk.*
19. *It's my birthday in a week.*
20. *We always rent a car when we travel.*

AUDIO 6.6 ◀◦))

VOCABULARY

Une balance nf | *A scale*
Une danse nf | *A dance*
Égoïste adj | *Selfish*
Malade adj | *Sick*
Elle pr | *She*
Je parle (Parler) v | *I am speaking (To speak)*
Je garde (Garder) v | *I am keeping (To keep)*
Il chante (Chanter) v | *He is singing (To sing)*
Elle marche (Marcher) v | *She is walking (To walk)*
On regarde (Regarder) v | *We are watching (To watch)*
On discute (Discuter) v | *We are talking (To talk)*
Me pr | *Me*
Une larme nf | *A tear*

Meilleur – Meilleure adj | *Best*
Une habitude nf | *A habit*
L'herbe nf | *Grass*
Arrêter v | *To stop*
Pousser v | *To grow*
Une semaine nf | *A week*
Jeune adj | *Young*
Choisir v | *To choose*
Éteindre v | *To turn off*
La télévision nf | *The television*
Quitter v | *To leave*
Une pièce nf | *A room*
Jaloux – Jalouse adj | *Jealous*
Un pull nm | *A sweater*
Large adj | *Big*
Tout le temps | *All the time*
Malade adj | *Sick*
Faire attention v | *Be careful – Watch out*
Une marche nf | *A step*
Une balade nf | *A walk*
La nature nf | *Nature*
Manger v | *To eat*
Une banane nf | *A banana*

Nécessaire adj | *Necessary*
Neiger v | *To snow*
Un matin nm | *A morning*
Planter v | *To plant*
Une carotte nf | *A carrot*
Perdre v | *To lose*
Une page nf | *A page*
Un livre nm | *A book*
Oublier v | *To forget*
Une écharpe nf | *A scarf*
Des travaux nm | *Work*
Une autoroute nf | *A highway*
Le temps nm | *Time*
Prendre v | *To have (drinks)*
Un café nm | *A coffee*
Le lait de soja nm | *Soy milk*
Préférer v | *To prefer*
Le lait d'amandes nm | *Almond milk*
Un anniversaire nm | *A birthday*
Une semaine nf | *A week*
Louer v | *To rent*
Une voiture nf | *A car*
Voyager v | *To travel*

LES TRABOULES DE LYON
THE TRABOULES OF LYON

7

AUDIO 7.1 🔊

> 1. **Écoutez l'audio** et **lisez l'histoire** en même temps.
>   *Listen to the audio and read the story at the same time.*

Les traboules de Lyon

Est-ce que vous savez qu'il y a des passages secrets dans la ville de Lyon ? Ces passages secrets s'appellent les traboules. Ce sont des passages qui relient deux rues à travers des maisons ou des immeubles. Elles existent depuis la Renaissance mais certaines sont plus récentes, du 18 et 19ème siècles. En gros, ce sont des raccourcis. Les habitants de Lyon les utilisent tous les jours et les touristes adorent les découvrir. Il y a plus de 500 traboules mais beaucoup d'entre elles sont fermées pour les préserver. Aujourd'hui, on peut encore en visiter 80. Les propriétaires peuvent décider de les fermer si les visiteurs posent des problèmes aux habitants du quartier. Si vous voulez découvrir les traboules, la meilleure façon c'est de prendre un guide. Un guide peut vous montrer toutes les traboules qui sont encore accessibles au public. Les visites sont en général pleines d'anecdotes et d'informations qui sont difficiles à trouver. Quand on visite une traboule, il faut être silencieux. Le bruit résonne dans les maisons et les immeubles. Il faut aussi les laisser comme on les a trouvées ; propres et sans trace de notre passage.

TRANSLATION

The Traboules of Lyon

Do you know that there are secret passages in the city of Lyon? These secret passages are called traboules. These are passages that connect two streets through houses or buildings. They have existed since the Renaissance, but some are more recent, dating back to the 18th and 19th centuries. Basically, they are shortcuts. The inhabitants of Lyon use them every day, and tourists love to discover them. There are more than 500 traboules, but many are closed to preserve them. Today, you can still visit 80 of them. The owners can decide to close them if the visitors cause problems for the residents of the neighborhood. If you want to discover the traboules, the best way is to take a guide. A guide can show you all the traboules that are still accessible to the public. The tours are generally full of anecdotes and information that is difficult to find. When you visit a traboule, you have to be silent. The noise echoes in houses and buildings. You must also leave them as you found them, clean and without a trace of your visit.

2. **Écoutez l'audio 7.1** et ajoutez **les mots manquants**.
Listen to the audio 7.1 and add the missing words.

Les traboules de Lyon

Est-ce que vous savez qu'il y a des   secrets dans la ville de Lyon ? Ces passages secrets s'appellent les traboules. Ce sont des passages qui relient deux   à travers des maisons ou des immeubles. Elles existent depuis la Renaissance mais certaines sont plus récentes, du 18 et 19ème   . En gros, ce sont des raccourcis. Les   de Lyon les utilisent tous les jours et les   adorent les découvrir. Il y a plus de 500 traboules mais beaucoup d'entre elles sont fermées pour les   . Aujourd'hui, on peut encore en visiter 80. Les propriétaires peuvent décider de les fermer si les   posent des problèmes aux habitants du quartier. Si vous voulez   les traboules, la meilleure façon c'est de prendre un guide. Un guide peut vous montrer toutes les traboules qui sont encore accessibles au   . Les visites sont en général pleines d'anecdotes et d'informations qui sont difficiles à   . Quand on visite une traboule, il faut être silencieux. Le bruit résonne dans les   et les immeubles. Il faut aussi les laisser comme on les a trouvées ; propres et sans   de notre passage.

AUDIO 7.2 🔊

VOCABULARY

Un passage secret nm + adj | *A secret passage*
Une ville nf | *A city*
S'appeler v | *To be called*
Une traboule nf | *A traboule*
Relier v | *To connect*
Une rue nf | *A street*
Une maison nf | *A house*
Un immeuble nm | *A building*
Exister v | *To exist*
La Renaissance nf | *The Renaissance*
Récent – Récente adj | *Recent*
Un raccourci nm | *A shortcut*
Un habitant – Une habitante n | *An inhabitant*
Un – Une touriste n | *A tourist*

Adorer v | *To love*
Découvrir v | *To discover*
Être fermé – fermée v | *To be closed*
Préserver v | *To preserve*
Un – Une propriétaire n | *The owners*
Décider v | *To decide*
Un visiteur – Une visiteuse n | *A visitor*
Poser des problèmes | *To cause problems*
Un quartier nm | *A neighborhood*
La meilleure façon adj + nf | *The best way*
Un – Une guide n | *A guide*
Montrer v | *To show*
Accessible adj | *Accessible*
Le public nm | *The public*

Une visite nf | *A visit*
Une anecdote nf | *An anecdote*
Une information nf | *Information*
Silencieux – Silencieuse adj | *Silent*
Le bruit nm | *Noise*

Résonner v | *To echo*
Laisser v | *To leave*
Propre adj | *Clean*
Une trace nf | *A trace*
Un passage nm | *A visit*

LE SON ON
THE SOUND ON

8

The sound **on** has two possible spellings in French. It's spelled **on** most of the time but it's spelled **om** before p or b, with the exception of "**Un bonbon** – *A candy*".

AUDIO 8.1 ◀)

on	**Une chanson** nf	*A song*
om before b and p	**Un pompier** nm	*A firefighter*

This exercise, "Listen and repeat," is divided into four different parts:

1. The sound only
2. The sound in syllables
3. The sound in words
4. Write down the words you hear

AUDIO 8.2 ◀)

1. Écoutez **le son on** et répétez après moi.
   *Listen to the sound **on** and repeat after me.*

   on – om

AUDIO 8.3 ◀)

2. Écoutez **le son on** dans **les différentes syllabes** et répétez après moi.
   *Listen to the sound **on** in the different syllables and repeat after me.*

   bon – don – fon – jon – lon – mon – non – pon – ron – son – ton – von – zon

AUDIO 8.4 ◀)

3. Écoutez **les différents mots** incluant le son **on** et répétez après moi.
   *Listen to the different words including the sound **on** and repeat after me.*

Un bonbon	**Un papillon**
Un dragon	**Un poisson**
Le monde	**Londres**
Une montagne	**Un monstre**
Un nom	**Un pont**

4. Écrivez **les mots** que vous entendez. Si vous ne comprenez pas le mot complet, écrivez une ou deux syllabes.
Write down the words you hear. If you don't understand the full word, write one or two syllables.

1.	Un	11.	Une
2.	Un	12.	
3.	Un	13.	Un
4.	Un	14.	Une
5.		15.	Une
6.		16.	Une
7.		17.	Une
8.	Un	18.	Une
9.	Une	19.	Un
10.	Un	20.	Un

VOCABULARY

Un bon nm | *A voucher*
Un bonbon nm | *A candy*
Un canon nm | *A cannon*
Un cochon nm | *A pig*
Un combat nm | *A fight*
Complet – Complète adj | *Complete*
Un dragon nm | *A dragon*
Fonder v | *To found*
Londres | *London*
Long – Longue adj | *Long*
Un menton nm | *A chin*
Le monde nm | *The world*
Un monstre nm | *A monster*
Une montagne nf | *A mountain*
Une montre nf | *A watch*

Un nom nm | *A name*
Un oncle nm | *An uncle*
Une opinion nf | *An opinion*
Pardon | *Pardon*
Un papillon nm | *A butterfly*
Un pigeon nm | *A pigeon*
Un poisson nm | *A fish*
Un pont nm | *A bridge*
Une potion nf | *A potion*
Une prison nf | *A prison*
Une question nf | *A question*
Une réunion nf | *A meeting*
Une saison nf | *A season*
Un son nm | *A sound*
Un talon nm | *A heel*

LE BUS N'EST PAS PASSÉ
THE BUS DID NOT COME

9

AUDIO 9.1 ◀))

1. **Écoutez l'audio** et **lisez l'histoire** en même temps.
   Listen to the audio and read the story at the same time.

Le bus n'est pas passé

Ce matin commence comme tous les autres matins pour Sarah. Elle se réveille à 6 heures, s'habille avant de quitter sa chambre et descend pour manger. Arrivée dans la cuisine, elle prépare son petit déjeuner. Elle mange la même chose tous les jours : deux tranches de pain avec de la confiture et un peu de beurre et une tasse de café. Une fois son petit déjeuner fini, elle va se brosser les dents et se maquiller. À 7 heures, elle part de la maison pour prendre son bus pour aller au travail. Elle arrive à l'arrêt de bus vers 7h10. Le bus arrive normalement à 7h15. Elle arrive toujours à la même heure et le bus est rarement en retard. Cinq minutes à attendre ce n'est pas beaucoup. Sarah attend et attend mais son bus n'arrive pas. Il est bientôt 7h30 et rien ! Son bus n'est pas passé. Elle va devoir appeler un taxi si elle veut arriver à l'heure au travail !

TRANSLATION

The Bus did not Come

This morning starts like every other morning for Sarah. She wakes up at 6 a.m., gets dressed before leaving her bedroom and goes downstairs to eat. Arriving in the kitchen, she prepares her breakfast. She eats the same thing every day: two slices of bread with jam, a little butter, and a cup of coffee. Once she finishes her breakfast, she goes to brush her teeth and put on makeup. At 7 a.m., she leaves the house to catch her bus to work. She arrives at the bus stop around 7:10 a.m. The bus arrives typically at 7:15 a.m. She always arrives at the same time, and the bus is rarely late. Five minutes of waiting isn't a lot. Sarah waits and waits, but her bus does not arrive. It's almost 7:30 a.m., and nothing! Her bus didn't come. She will have to call a taxi if she wants to get to work on time!

2. Écoutez l'audio 9.1 et **numérotez les phrases de 1 à 14 pour les remettre dans l'ordre.**
Listen to the audio 9.1 and number the sentences from 1 to 14 to put them in order.

– Elle va devoir appeler un taxi si elle veut arriver à l'heure au travail !

– Arrivée dans la cuisine, elle prépare son petit déjeuner.

– Elle arrive toujours à la même heure et le bus est rarement en retard.

– Sarah attend et attend mais son bus n'arrive pas.

– Une fois son petit déjeuner fini, elle va se brosser les dents et se maquiller.

– Elle arrive à l'arrêt de bus vers 7h10.

– Ce matin commence comme tous les autres matins pour Sarah.

– Le bus arrive normalement à 7h15.

– Cinq minutes à attendre ce n'est pas beaucoup.

– À 7 heures, elle part de la maison pour prendre son bus pour aller au travail.

– Elle se réveille à 6 heures, s'habille avant de quitter sa chambre et descend pour manger.

– Il est bientôt 7h30 et rien !

– Elle mange la même chose tous les jours : deux tranches de pain avec de la confiture et un peu de beurre et une tasse de café.

– Son bus n'est pas passé.

AUDIO 9.2 🔊

VOCABULARY

Un bus nm | *A bus*
Passer v | *To come (for transportation)*
Commencer v | *To start*
Se réveiller v | *To wake up*
S'habiller v | *To get dressed*
Quitter v | *To leave*
Une chambre nf | *A bedroom*
Descendre v | *To go downstairs*

Un petit déjeuner nm | *A breakfast*
Une cuisine nf | *A kitchen*
Préparer v | *To prepare*
Manger v | *To eat*
Une tasse de café nf | *A cup of coffee*
Une tranche de pain nf | *A slice of bread*
De la confiture nf | *Jam*
Du beurre nm | *Butter*

Se brosser les dents v | *To brush your teeth*
Se maquiller v | *To put on makeup*
Prendre son bus v | *To catch a bus*
Un arrêt de bus nm | *A bus stop*
En retard adv | *Late*
Attendre v | *To wait*

Arriver v | *To arrive*
Appeler v | *To call*
Un taxi nm | *A taxi*
À l'heure adv | *On time*
Le travail nm | *Work*

UNE SEMAINE À LA MONTAGNE
A WEEK IN THE MOUNTAINS

10

AUDIO 10.1 ◀))

1. **Écoutez l'audio** et **lisez l'histoire** en même temps.
   Listen to the audio and read the story at the same time.

Une semaine à la montagne

Steve   – Tu es prête pour notre semaine à la montagne ?

Camille – Presque ! Je dois encore faire ma valise.

Steve   – Tu as trouvé ton passeport ?

Camille – Oui, il était resté dans mon sac après notre dernier voyage. Encore heureux car je ne sais pas ce que j'aurais fait si je ne l'avais pas trouvé. Et toi, tu es prêt ?

Steve   – Oui, je viens de finir ma valise. J'ai encore quelques habits à laver mais c'est tout. Je dois aussi aller au magasin pour acheter des barres protéinées pour nos randonnées. Je suis sûr qu'on peut en trouver là-bas mais on ne sait jamais.

Camille – En parlant d'achats, est-ce que tu as reçu tes nouvelles chaussures de marche ?

Steve   – Oui mais elles n'étaient pas confortables du tout donc je les ai renvoyées. Mes vieilles chaussures sont encore en bon état donc je les garde pour cette saison.

Camille – C'est dommage. On devrait regarder près de l'hôtel. Il y a souvent des magasins de sport dans les villages de montagne.

Steve   – C'est vrai. On peut regarder là-bas. On se rejoint à l'aéroport samedi matin à neuf heures ?

Camille – Ok. Je t'écris quand je pars de chez moi. J'ai hâte. À samedi !

Steve   – À samedi !

TRANSLATION

A Week in the Mountains

Steve   – *Are you ready for our week in the mountains?*

Camille – *Almost! I still have to pack my suitcase.*

Steve   – *Did you find your passport?*

Camille – *Yes, it was left in my bag after our last trip. I am glad I found it because I don't know what I would have done if I hadn't. And you, are you ready?*

Steve	–	Yes, I just finished my suitcase. I still have a few clothes to wash, but that's it. I also have to go to the store to buy protein bars for our hikes. I'm sure we can find some there, but you never know.
Camille	–	Speaking of purchases, have you got your new walking shoes?
Steve	–	Yes, but they weren't comfortable at all, so I sent them back. My old shoes are still in good condition, so I'm keeping them for this season.
Camille	–	It's a shame. We should look near the hotel. There are often sports shops in mountain villages.
Steve	–	That's right. We can look there. Are we meeting at the airport at nine on Saturday morning?
Camille	–	Ok. I'll text you when I leave home. I can't wait! See you Saturday!
Steve	–	See you Saturday!

2. **Écoutez l'audio une nouvelle fois** et ajoutez **le nom de la personne** à côté des faits listés.
Listen to the audio again and add the person's name next to the facts listed.

1. Qui doit encore faire sa valise ?
Who still needs to pack?

2. Qui a perdu son passeport ?
Who lost their passport?

3. Qui doit encore laver quelques habits ?
Who still has to wash some clothes?

4. Qui doit acheter des barres protéinées ?
Who has to buy protein bars?

5. Qui a reçu ses nouvelles chaussures de marche ?
Who received their new walking shoes?

6. Qui propose de faire du shopping près de l'hôtel ?
Who offers to go shopping near the hotel?

7. Qui dit de se rejoindre à neuf heures à l'aéroport ?
Who says to meet at nine o'clock at the airport?

8. Qui va écrire à l'autre avant de partir ?
Who will text the other before leaving?

VOCABULARY

Une semaine nf | *A week*

La montagne nf | *The mountain*

Prêt – Prête adj | *Ready*

Une valise nf | *A suitcase*

Un passeport nm | *A passport*

Un sac nm | *A bag*

Le dernier voyage adj + nm | *The last trip*

Trouver v | *To find*

Finir v | *To finish*

Un habit nm | *A piece of clothing*

Laver v | *To wash*

Un magasin nm | *A store*

Acheter v | *To buy*

Une barre protéinée nf | *A protein bar*

Une randonnée nf | *A hike*

Un achat nm | *A purchase*

Nouveau – Nouvelle adj | *New*

Des chaussures de marche nf | *Walking shoes*

Confortable adj | *Comfortable*

Renvoyer v | *To send back*

Vieux – Vieille adj | *Old*

Garder v | *To keep*

Une saison nf | *A season*

Dommage adj | *Too bad*

Un hôtel nm | *A hotel*

Un magasin de sport nm | *A sport shop*

Un village nm | *A village*

Regarder v | *To look*

Se rejoindre v | *To meet*

Un aéroport nm | *An airport*

Samedi nm | *Saturday*

Écrire v | *To text*

Partir v | *To leave*

LA CABANE DANS LE JARDIN
THE SHED IN THE GARDEN

11

AUDIO 11.1 ◀ⁱ))

1. **Écoutez l'audio** et **lisez l'histoire** en même temps.
   Listen to the audio and read the story at the same time.

La cabane dans le jardin

Dans le jardin de mes parents, il y a une vieille cabane. C'est une cabane en bois avec un toit en métal. Avec mes frères, on y jouait souvent quand on était petits. Elle semblait énorme quand on y jouait mais maintenant que je suis adulte, elle a l'air minuscule. Je suis un peu nostalgique car mes parents vont la détruire bientôt. Ils disent qu'elle est en mauvais état et qu'ils ne s'en servent pas. C'est vrai qu'elle est vide. Il n'y a rien à l'intérieur. Les tempêtes de l'année dernière ont abîmé la porte et les fenêtres. Mes parents disent que ce n'est pas la peine de la réparer. Ils disent que cela coûterait trop cher. Je suis d'accord avec eux mais je suis un peu triste qu'elle soit démolie. Je pense que je vais garder quelques planches. Peut-être que je les utiliserai pour faire un meuble, un plateau, ou peut-être juste un cadre. Ça sera une chouette façon de garder un souvenir de notre cabane.

TRANSLATION

The Shed in the Garden

In my parents' garden, there is an old shed. It is a wooden shed with a metal roof. My brothers and I often played there when we were little. It seemed huge when we played, but now that I'm an adult, it looks tiny. I'm a little nostalgic because my parents are going to tear it down soon. They say it's in bad condition and they don't use it. It's true that it is empty. There is nothing inside. Last year's storms damaged the door and windows. My parents say there's no need to repair it. They say it would cost too much. I agree with them, but I'm a little sad that it's being demolished. I think I'll keep a few boards. Maybe I'll use them to make a piece of furniture, a tray, or maybe just a frame. It will be a nice way to keep a souvenir of our shed.

2. **Écoutez l'audio 11.1** et ajoutez **les mots manquants**.
Listen to the audio 11.1 and add the missing words.

La cabane dans le jardin

Dans le jardin de mes _____, il y a une vieille cabane. C'est une cabane en bois avec un toit en _____. Avec mes frères, on y jouait souvent quand on était petits. Elle semblait énorme quand on y jouait mais maintenant que je suis _____, elle a l'air minuscule. Je suis un peu _____ car mes parents vont la détruire bientôt. Ils disent qu'elle est en mauvais état et qu'ils ne s'en servent pas. C'est _____ qu'elle est vide. Il n'y a rien à l'intérieur. Les _____ de l'année dernière ont abîmé la _____ et les fenêtres. Mes parents disent que ce n'est pas la peine de la _____. Ils disent que cela coûterait trop _____. Je suis d'accord avec eux mais je suis un peu _____ qu'elle soit démolie. Je pense que je vais garder quelques planches. Peut-être que je les utiliserai pour faire un meuble, un plateau, ou peut-être juste un _____. Ça sera une chouette façon de garder un _____ de notre cabane.

AUDIO 11.2 ◄))

VOCABULARY

Le jardin nm | *The garden*
Les parents nm | *Parents*
Une vieille cabane adj + nf | *An old shed*
Du bois nm | *Wood*
Un toit nm | *A roof*
Du métal nm | *Metal*
Un frère nm | *A brother*
Jouer v | *To play*
Petit – Petite adj | *Small*
Sembler v | *To seem*
Énorme adj | *Huge*
Un – Une adulte n | *An adult*
Minuscule adj | *Tiny*
Nostalgique adj | *Nostalgic*
Détruire v | *To tear down*
En mauvais état adj | *In bad shape*
Se servir v | *To use*
Vide adj | *Empty*

À l'intérieur adv | *Inside*
Une tempête nf | *A storm*
L'année dernière nf + adj | *Last year*
Abîmer v | *To damage*
Une porte nf | *A door*
Une fenêtre nf | *A window*
Réparer v | *To repair*
Coûter v | *To cost*
Cher – Chère adj | *Expensive*
Triste adj | *Sad*
Être démoli(e) v | *To be demolished*
Garder v | *To keep*
Une planche nf | *A board*
Un meuble nm | *A piece of furniture*
Un plateau nm | *A tray*
Un cadre nm | *A frame*
Une chouette façon nf + adj | *A nice way*
Un souvenir nm | *A souvenir*

LES SONS IN – AN – ON
THE SOUNDS IN – AN – ON

12

In Chapter 2, you have learned to recognize **the sound in**, **the sound an** in Chapter 4, and **the sound on** in Chapter 8, it's time to review them together in an exercise!

Here are the different spellings for each sound:

The Sound in

in – im – ain – aim – ein – yn – ym – un – um

The Sound an

an – am – en – am – aon

The Sound on

on – om

AUDIO 12.1 ◄))

Écoutez **les différentes phrases** et ajoutez **le bon son** à chaque partie manquante.
Listen to the different sentences and add the correct sound to each missing part.

1. Je dois me ch   ger av   t de partir.

2.   habite à la m   tagne.

3. Le sal   de coiffure sera fermé ce dim   che.

4.   peut m   ger m   ten   t si tu as f   .

5. Ma fille a r   dez-vous chez le d   tiste l   di proch   .

6. Le t   ps est frais   automne.

7. J'aime pr   dre b   qu   d j'ai froid.

8. C'est   possible de résoudre ce problème.

9. Beaucoup préfère le v   bl   c au v   rouge.

10. Il y a pl   de dess   s accrochés au frigo.

---

11. J'ai p   t ma ch   bre   bl   c.

12. Est-ce que tu peux baisser le s   ?

13. Les pige   s att   dent de recevoir du p   .

14. M   cle ne sera pas là à notre mariage.

15. Le cli   t a r   pli le c   trat.

TRANSLATION

1. *I have to change before leaving.*

2. *We live in the mountains.*

3. *The hair salon will be closed this Sunday.*

4. *We can eat now if you are hungry.*

5. *My daughter has a dentist appointment next Monday.*

6. *The weather is cool in the fall.*

7. *I like to take a bath when I'm cold.*

8. *This problem cannot be resolved.*

9. *Many prefer white wine to red wine.*

10. *There are lots of drawings hanging on the fridge.*

11. *I painted my bedroom white.*

12. *Can you turn down the sound?*

13. *The pigeons are waiting to get bread.*

14. *My uncle won't be there at our wedding.*

15. *The customer has fulfilled the contract.*

AUDIO 12.2 ◀))

VOCABULARY

Se changer v | *To change*
Avant adv | *Before*
Partir v | *To leave*
Habiter v | *To live*
Une montagne nf | *A mountain*
Un salon de coiffure nm | *A hair salon*
Le dimanche nm | *Sunday*
On pr | *We*
Manger v | *To eat*

Maintenant adv | *Now*
Avoir faim v | *To be hungry*
Un rendez-vous nm | *An appointment*
Un dentiste nm | *A dentist*
Le lundi nm | *Monday*
Prochain – Prochaine adj | *Next*
Le temps nm | *The weather*
Frais – Fraîche adj | *Cool*
En automne | *In the fall*

Prendre v | *To take*
Un bain nm | *A bath*
Quand adv | *When*
Avoir froid v | *To be cold*
Impossible adj | *Impossible*
Résoudre v | *To resolve*
Un problème nm | *A problem*
Préférer v | *To prefer*
Du vin blanc nm | *White wine*
Du vin rouge nm | *Red wine*
Plein – Pleine adj | *Full*
Un dessin nm | *A drawing*
Accrocher v | *To hang*
Un frigo nm | *A fridge*

Peindre v | *To paint*
Une chambre nf | *A bedroom*
Blanc – Blanche adj | *White*
Baisser v | *To lower*
Le son nm | *The sound*
Un pigeon nm | *A pigeon*
Attendre v | *To wait*
Recevoir v | *To get*
Du pain nm | *Bread*
Un oncle nm | *An uncle*
Un mariage nm | *A wedding*
Un client nm | *A client*
Remplir v | *To fulfill*
Un contrat nm | *A contract*

MA JOURNÉE DE CONGÉ
MY DAY OFF

13

AUDIO 13.1 🔊

1. **Écoutez l'audio** et **lisez l'histoire** en même temps.
   Listen to the audio and read the story at the same time.

Ma journée de congé

J'aime être productif pendant ma journée de congé. Je commence souvent par faire un peu de rangement et un peu de ménage. Je lave aussi les draps de lit et les serviettes de bain. Pendant que la machine à laver fait son travail, je regarde ce que j'ai dans le frigo et les placards de la cuisine pour les repas de la semaine. Une fois que j'ai fait ma liste de courses, je vais au magasin pour faire mes courses. Sur le chemin du retour, je m'arrête à la pompe à essence pour faire le plein. Quand je rentre, je mets les draps et les serviettes dans le sèche-linge et je range les courses. Après ça, je fais une heure de sport avant de me doucher. Si j'ai faim, je prépare le dîner, sinon, je lis un bon livre pendant une heure ou deux. Si je ne suis pas productif, j'ai l'impression de perdre mon temps. Une journée bien remplie, pour moi, c'est toujours une bonne journée.

TRANSLATION

My Day Off

I like to be productive on my day off. I often start by doing a little tidying and cleaning. I also wash the bed sheets and bath towels. While the washing machine does its job, I look at what I have in the fridge and kitchen cupboards for this week's meals. Once I make my shopping list, I go to the store to do my shopping. On the way back, I stop at the gas station to fill up. When I get home, I put the sheets and towels in the dryer and put the groceries away. After that, I exercise for an hour before showering. If I'm hungry, I cook dinner, if not, I read a good book for an hour or two. If I'm not productive, I feel like I'm wasting my time. A busy day, for me, is always a good day.

2. **Écoutez l'audio 13.1** et **numérotez les phrases de 1 à 11 pour les remettre dans l'ordre.**
   Listen to the audio 13.1 and number the sentences from 1 to 11 to put them in order.

   – Une journée bien remplie, pour moi, c'est toujours une bonne journée.

   – Quand je rentre, je mets les draps et les serviettes dans le sèche-linge et je range les courses.

– J'aime être productif pendant ma journée de congé.

– Sur le chemin du retour, je m'arrête à la pompe à essence pour faire le plein.

– Je lave aussi les draps de lit et les serviettes de bain.

– Une fois que j'ai fait ma liste de courses, je vais au magasin pour faire mes courses.

– Pendant que la machine à laver fait son travail, je regarde ce que j'ai dans le frigo et les placards de la cuisine pour les repas de la semaine.

– Si j'ai faim, je prépare le dîner, sinon, je lis un bon livre pendant une heure ou deux.

– Je commence souvent par faire un peu de rangement et un peu de ménage.

– Si je ne suis pas productif, j'ai l'impression de perdre mon temps.

– Après ça, je fais une heure de sport avant de me doucher.

AUDIO 13.2 ◀))

VOCABULARY

Une journée de congé nf | *A day off*
Productif – Productive adj | *Productive*
Commencer v | *To start*
Du rangement nm | *Tidying*
Le ménage nm | *Cleaning*
Laver v | *To wash*
Un drap de lit nm | *A bed sheet*
Une serviette de bain nf | *A bath towel*
Une machine à laver nf | *A washing machine*
Un frigo nm | *A fridge*
Un placard nm | *A cupboard*
Un repas nm | *A meal*
Une liste de courses nf | *A shopping list*
Un magasin nm | *A store*
Faire les courses v | *Grocery shopping*

Le chemin du retour nm | *The way back*
S'arrêter v | *To stop*
La pompe à essence nf | *The gas station*
Faire le plein v | *To fill up*
Un sèche-linge nm | *A dryer*
Faire du sport nm | *To exercise*
Se doucher v | *To shower*
Le dîner nm | *Dinner*
Lire v | *To read*
Un bon livre adj + nm | *A good book*
Avoir l'impression v | *To feel like*
Perdre son temps v | *To waste time*
Rempli – Remplie adj | *Busy*

LE SON EUILLE
THE SOUND EUILLE

14

The sound **euille** has five possible spellings in French. It's spelled **euil** and **euille** most of the time but it's spelled **ueil** and **ueille** after **c** or **g**, and the spelling **œil** which is the one for the word "**Un œil** – *An eye.*"

Not many words include this sound in French but it's one worth practicing. This is why this lesson doesn't include a lot of vocabulary.

AUDIO 14.1 ◄))

euill(e)	**Une f<u>euille</u>** nf | *A leaf*
euil	**Un écur<u>euil</u>** nm | *A squirrel*
ueil after c and g	**Un acc<u>ueil</u>** nm | *A welcome*
ueill(e) after c and g	**C<u>ueil</u>lir** v | *To pick*
œil	**Un <u>œil</u>** nm | *An eye*

This exercise, "Listen and repeat," is divided into four different parts:

1. The sound only
2. The sound in syllables
3. The sound in words
4. Put the words in order

AUDIO 14.2 ◄))

1. Écoutez **le son euille** et répétez après moi.
   *Listen to the sound **euille** and repeat after me.*

→ *A good way to explain this sound is to pronounce **e** + the beginning of "**yes**" in English. I like to explain as **e** + a rolling y.*

   euil – euille – ueil – ueille – œil

AUDIO 14.3 ◄))

2. Écoutez **le son euille** dans **les différentes syllabes** et répétez après moi.
   *Listen to the sound **euille** in the different syllables and repeat after me.*

   beuille – deuille – feuille – jeuille – leuille – meuille – neuille – peuille – reuille – seuille – teuille – veuille – zeuille

3. Écoutez **les différents mots** incluant le son **euille** et répétez après moi.
   *Listen to the different words including the sound **euille** and repeat after me.*

Un acc**ueil**   Un faut**euil**
Acc**ueil**lir   Une f**euille**
Un cerc**ueil**   Un millef**euille**
Un chevr**euil**   Un **œil**
C**ueil**lir   L'org**ueil**
Le d**euil**   Un portef**euille**
Un écur**euil**   Le s**euil**

4. Écoutez **l'audio** et remettez **les mots dans l'ordre**.
   Listen to the audio and put the words in order.

Un accueil

Accueillir

Un cercueil

Un chevreuil

Cueillir

Le deuil

Un écureuil

Un fauteuil

Une feuille

Un millefeuille

Un œil

L'orgueil

Un portefeuille

Le seuil

VOCABULARY

Un accueil nm | *A welcome*

Accueillir v | *To welcome*

Un cercueil nm | *A coffin*

Un chevreuil nm | *A deer*

Cueillir v | *To pick*

Le deuil nm | *Mourning*

Un écureuil nm | *A squirrel*

Un fauteuil nm | *An armchair*

Une feuille nf | *A leaf*

Un millefeuille nm | *A mille-feuille (pastry)*

Un œil nm | *An eye*

L'orgueil nm | *Pride*

Un portefeuille nm | *A wallet*

Le seuil nm | *The threshold*

QUEL MOT EST-CE QUE JE PRONONCE ? 15
WHAT WORD DO I PRONOUNCE?

Écoutez **l'audio** et **entourez** le mot que je prononce. Chaque mot est répété deux fois. La liste des mots est traduite après cet exercice.
Listen to the audio and circle the word I say. Each word is repeated twice. The list of words is translated after this exercise.

1. Ventre – Vendre
2. Note – Notre
3. Fleur – Peur
4. Pour – Pur
5. Peau – Peu
6. Roule – Rouge
7. Gros – Gras
8. Marche – Marché
9. Banc – Blanc
10. Lu – Loup
11. Moi – Moine
12. Bois – Boîte
13. Faux – Feu
14. Attendre – Entendre
15. Sol – Sale
16. Nous – Nu
17. Bague – Blague
18. Bras – Bas
19. Brise – Bise
20. Courir – Nourrir

AUDIO 15.2

VOCABULARY

Le ventre nm | *The belly*
Vendre v | *To sell*
Une note nf | *A note*
Notre pr | *Our*
Une fleur nf | *A flower*
Une peur nf | *A fear*
Pour prep | *For*
Pur – Pure adj | *Pure*
La peau nf | *The skin*
Un peu adj | *A little*
Roule (Rouler) v | *To roll*
Rouge adj | *Red*
Gros – Grosse adj | *Big*
Gras – Grasse adj | *Fat – Oily*
Une marche nf | *A step*
Un marché nf | *A market*
Un banc nm | *A bench*
Blanc – Blanche adj | *White*
Lu pp | *Read*
Un loup nm | *A wolf*

Moi pr | *Me*
Un moine nm | *A monk*
Le bois nm | *Wood*
Une boîte nf | *A box*
Faux – Fausse adj | *False*
Un feu nm | *A fire*
Attendre v | *To wait*
Entendre v | *To hear*
Le sol nm | *The floor*
Sale adj | *Dirty*
Nous pr | *We*
Nu – Nue adj | *Naked*
Une bague nf | *A ring*
Une blague nf | *A joke*
Un bras nm | *An arm*
Un bas nm | *A stocking*
Une brise nf | *A breeze*
Une bise nf | *A kiss*
Courir v | *To run*
Nourrir v | *To feed*

LA LETTRE MUETTE S
THE SILENT LETTER S

16

What is a Silent Letter?

A silent letter in French is a letter that is not pronounced. A silent letter is usually at the end of a word.

The letter **s** is often silent in different types of words. It's one of the most common silent letters after **e**.

Here are the four types of words where you can find the silent letter **s** in French:

AUDIO 16.1 ◄))

At the end of nouns, adjectives and pronouns when they are plural

Une lampe – Des lampes nf | *A lamp – Lamps*
Un chat – Des chats nm | *A cat – Cats*

Propre – Propres adj | *Clean*
Calme – Calmes adj | *Calm*

Il – Ils pr | *He – They*
Elle – Elles pr | *She – They*

AUDIO 16.2 ◄))

At the end of specific nouns (not plural), prepositions, and adverbs

Une souris nf | *A mouse*
Un bras nm | *An arm*
Un tapis nm | *A carpet*

Sous prep | *Under*
Dans prep | *In*

Alors adv | *Then*
Après adv | *After*

When a verb is conjugated with je – tu – nous

Je dis v | *I say*
Je comprends v | *I understand*
Je finis v | *I finish*

Tu parles v | *You are speaking*
Tu chantes v | *You are singing*
Tu t'appelles v | *You are named*

Nous voyons v | *We see*
Nous faisons v | *We are doing*
Nous dansons v | *We are dancing*

At the end of different negations

ne ... pas | *not*
ne ... plus | *no more*
ne ... jamais | *never*

Note that -es in articles and adjectives make a specific sound and are not considered as a silent letter

mes adj | *my*
tes adj | *your*
ces adj | *these*
ses adj | *his – her*
les art | *the*
des art | *some*

1. Écoutez la différence lorsque **la lettre s** est **prononcée** et **non prononcée**.
   *Listen to the difference when the letter **s** is pronounced and not pronounced.*

Un bus – *A bus*
Un bois – *Wood*

2. Écoutez ces 20 phrases et **entourez les mots** où **la lettre s est muette**.
*Listen to these 20 sentences and circle the words where the letter **s** is silent.*

1. Le mois de février a 28 jours.
2. Le repas sera servi dans deux heures.
3. Il s'est fait mal au dos en déplaçant ces boîtes.
4. Le bois derrière chez moi me fait toujours peur.
5. Mon colis devrait être livré ce matin.
6. Je n'ai jamais vu ce film.
7. Cela vaut moins que cent euros.
8. Qu'est-ce que tu fais ce soir ?
9. Je dors souvent tard le samedi.
10. Le ciel est gris aujourd'hui.
11. Apprendre le français peut être difficile.
12. Ce documentaire est très intéressant.
13. Je viendrai au repas sans mon mari.
14. Tes dessins sont vraiment jolis.
15. Les jours sont courts en hiver.
16. Il fait mauvais depuis une semaine.
17. Je trie mes habits en hiver et en été.
18. Il n'y a plus de pain chez le boulanger.
19. Mon chien a des taches brunes sur le corps.
20. Ils n'ont pas besoin d'être présents à la réunion.

TRANSLATION

1. *The month of February has 28 days.*
2. *The meal will be served in two hours.*
3. *He hurt his back moving those boxes.*
4. *The woods behind my house always scare me.*
5. *My package should be delivered this morning.*
6. *I have never seen this film.*
7. *It's worth less than a hundred euros.*
8. *What are you doing tonight?*
9. *I often sleep late on Saturdays.*

10. *The sky is gray today.*

11. *Learning French can be difficult.*

12. *This documentary is very interesting.*

13. *I will come to the meal without my husband.*

14. *Your drawings are really pretty.*

15. *The days are short in winter.*

16. *The weather has been bad for a week.*

17. *I sort my clothes in winter and summer.*

18. *There is no more bread at the baker.*

19. *My dog has brown spots on his body.*

20. *They do not need to be present at the meeting.*

AUDIO 16.8 🔊

VOCABULARY

Une lampe nf | *A lamp*
Un chat nm | *A cat*
Propre adj | *Clean*
Calme adj | *Calm*
Il pr | *He*
Ils pr | *They*
Elle pr | *She*
Elles pr | *They*
Une souris nf | *A mouse*
Un bras nm | *An arm*
Un tapis nm | *A carpet*
Sous prep | *Under*
Dans prep | *In*
Alors adv | *Then*
Après adv | *After*
Je dis (Dire) v | *I say (To say)*
Je comprends (Comprendre) v | *I understand (To understand)*
Je finis (Finir) v | *I finish (To finish)*
Tu parles (Parler) v | *I am speaking (To speak)*
Tu chantes (Chanter) v | *You are singing (To sing)*
Tu t'appelles (S'appeler) v | *You are named (To be named)*
Nous voyons (Voir) v | *We see (To see)*

Nous faisons (Faire) v | *We are doing (To do)*
Nous dansons (Danser) v | *We are dancing (To dance)*
Ne ... pas | *Not*
Ne ... plus | *No more*
Ne ... jamais | *Never*
Mes adj | *My*
Tes adj | *Your*
Ces adj | *These*
Ses adj | *His – Her*
Les art | *The*
Des art | *Some*
Un bus nm | *A bus*
Un bois nm | *Wood*
Un mois nm | *A month*
Février nm | *February*
Un jour nm | *A day*
Un repas nm | *A meal*
Se faire mal v | *To hurt yourself*
Le dos nm | *The back*
Une boîte nf | *A box*
Derrière adv | *Behind*
Faire peur v | *To scare*
Un colis nm | *A package*
Le matin nm | *The morning*

Jamais adv | *Never*
Un film nm | *A film*
Valoir v | *To be worth*
Moins adv | *Less*
Un euro nm | *A euro*
Ce soir nm | *Tonight*
Dormir v | *To sleep*
Tard adv | *Late*
Le samedi nm | *Saturday*
Le ciel nm | *The sky*
Gris – Grise adj | *Gray*
Apprendre v | *To learn*
Le français nm | *French*
Difficile adj | *Difficult*
Un documentaire nm | *A documentary*
Intéressant – Intéressante adj | *Interesting*
Un repas nm | *A meal*
Sans prep | *Without*
Un mari nm | *A husband*

Un dessin nm | *A drawing*
Joli – Jolie adj | *Pretty*
Un jour nm | *A day*
Court – Courte adj | *Short*
L'hiver nm | *Winter*
Faire mauvais v | *To be bad (weather)*
Une semaine nf | *A week*
Trier v | *To sort*
Un habit nm | *A piece of clothing*
L'été nm | *Summer*
Un pain nm | *A loaf of bread*
Le boulanger nm | *The baker*
Un chien nm | *A dog*
Une tache nf | *A spot*
Brun – Brune adj | *Brown*
Un corps nm | *A body*
Présent – Présente adj | *Present*
Une réunion nf | *A meeting*

LE MARCHÉ DU DIMANCHE
THE SUNDAY MARKET

17

1. **Écoutez l'audio** et **lisez l'histoire** en même temps.
   Listen to the audio and read the story at the same time.

Le marché du dimanche

Dans le petit village de Valmont-aux-Bois, il y a un marché tous les dimanches matin. C'est un marché en plein air, dans les rues de la vieille ville. Une cinquantaine de vendeurs viennent de toute la province pour vendre leurs produits. Ils arrivent tôt pour avoir les meilleures places. Certains arrivent à 5 heures du matin. Ils s'installent et commencent à décharger leur camion directement. Il y a beaucoup de choses à faire avant que les premiers clients arrivent à 7 heures. Techniquement, il n'y a pas d'heure d'ouverture mais c'est rare que les gens arrivent avant 7 heures. On peut tout acheter au marché : des fruits, des légumes, des épices, de la viande, du poisson, des œufs, des fleurs, des habits et même de la décoration pour la maison. Les clients sont souvent les mêmes et ils achètent presque toujours la même chose. Quand il fait beau, c'est un vrai plaisir de se promener dans les rues en faisant ses courses. Quand il pleut par contre, ce n'est pas très gai. Même les vendeurs savent qu'ils vendront moins si le temps n'est pas bon.

TRANSLATION

The Sunday Market

In the small village of Valmont-aux-Bois, there is a market every Sunday morning. It is an open-air market, in the streets of the old town. Around fifty vendors come from across the province to sell their products. They arrive early to get the best places. Some arrive at 5 a.m. They settle in and start unloading their truck straight away. There is a lot to do before the first customers arrive at 7 o'clock. Technically, there is no opening time but it's rare that people arrive before 7 a.m. You can buy everything at the market: fruits, vegetables, spices, meat, fish, eggs, flowers, clothes and even decorations for the house. The customers are often the same and they almost always buy the same thing. When the weather is nice, it's a real pleasure to walk the streets while doing your shopping. When it rains, however, it's not very pleasant. Even the sellers know that they will sell less if the weather is not good.

2. **Écoutez l'audio 17.1** et ajoutez **les mots manquants**.
Listen to the audio 17.1 and add the missing words.

Le marché du dimanche

Dans le petit _____ de Valmont-aux-Bois, il y a un marché tous les dimanches _____ . C'est un marché en plein air, dans les _____ de la vieille ville. Une cinquantaine de vendeurs viennent de toute la _____ pour vendre leurs produits. Ils arrivent tôt pour avoir les meilleures _____ . Certains arrivent à 5 heures du matin. Ils s'installent et commencent à décharger leur _____ directement. Il y a beaucoup de _____ à faire avant que les premiers clients arrivent à 7 heures. Techniquement, il n'y a pas d'heure d'ouverture mais c'est rare que les gens arrivent avant 7 heures. On peut tout acheter au marché : des fruits, des _____ , des épices, de la viande, du poisson, des œufs, des _____ , des habits et même de la décoration pour la _____ . Les clients sont souvent les mêmes et ils achètent presque toujours la même chose. Quand il fait _____ , c'est un vrai plaisir de se promener dans les rues en faisant ses courses. Quand il pleut par contre, ce n'est pas très gai. Même les vendeurs savent qu'ils vendront moins si le _____ n'est pas bon.

AUDIO 17.2 ◀))

VOCABULARY

Un petit village adj + nm | *A small village*
Un marché nm | *A market*
Le dimanche nm | *Sunday*
Le matin nm | *Morning*
En plein air adv | *Open-air*
Une rue nf | *A street*
La vieille ville adj + nf | *The old town*
Un vendeur – Une vendeuse n | *A vendor*
Une province nf | *A province*
Vendre v | *To sell*
Un produit nm | *A product*
Arriver v | *To arrive*
Tôt adv | *Early*
La meilleure place adj + nf | *The best place*
S'installer v | *To settle in*

Décharger v | *To unload*
Un camion nm | *A truck*
Une chose nf | *A thing*
Un client – Une cliente n | *A customer*
L'heure d'ouverture nf | *Opening time*
Rare adj | *Rare*
Les gens nm | *People*
Acheter v | *To buy*
Des fruits nm | *Fruits*
Des légumes nm | *Vegetables*
Des épices nf | *Spices*
De la viande nf | *Meat*
Du poisson nm | *Fish*
Des œufs nm | *Eggs*
Des fleurs nf | *Flowers*

Des habits nm | *Clothes*

De la décoration nf | *Decorations*

Faire beau v | *To be nice*

Un vrai plaisir adj + nm | *A real pleasure*

Se promener v | *To walk*

Une rue nf | *A street*

Faire les courses v | *To do the shopping*

Pleuvoir v | *To rain*

Gai – Gaie adj | *Pleasant*

Bon – Bonne adj | *Good*

LE SON EILLE
THE SOUND EILLE

18

The sound **eille** has two possible spellings in French. It's spelled **eil** and **eille**.

AUDIO 18.1 ◄ »

eil
eill(e)

Un cons<u>eil</u> nm | An advice
Une ab<u>eille</u> nf | A bee

When the sound **eille** is at the end of a noun, masculine nouns end in **eil**, feminine nouns end in **eille**.

This exercise, "Listen and repeat," is divided into four different parts:

1. The sound only
2. The sound in syllables
3. The sound in words
4. Write down the words you hear

AUDIO 18.2 ◄ »

1. Écoutez **le son eille** et répétez après moi.
   *Listen to the sound **eille** and repeat after me.*

→ *A good way to explain this sound is to pronounce **é** + the beginning of "yes" in English. I like to explain as é + a rolling y.*

eil – eille

AUDIO 18.3 ◄ »

2. Écoutez **le son eille** dans **les différentes syllabes** et répétez après moi.
   *Listen to the **eille** sound in the different syllables and repeat after me.*

beille – ceille – deille – feille – jeille – leille – meille – neille – peille – reille – seille – teille – veille – zeille

---

3. Écoutez **les différents mots** incluant le son **eille** et répétez après moi.
   *Listen to the different words including the sound **eille** and repeat after me.*

Un appar**eil**
Un cons**eil**
Une corn**eille**
Une gros**eille**
Mars**eille**

Une or**eille**
Un ort**eil**
Un rév**eil**
Le somm**eil**
Vi**eille**

4. Écrivez **les mots** que vous entendez. Si vous ne comprenez pas le mot complet, écrivez une ou deux syllabes.
   Write down the words you hear. If you don't understand the full word, write one or two syllables.

1. Une

2. Une

3.

4. Une

5.

6. Un

7.

8. Se

9. Le

10.

VOCABULARY

Une abeille nf | *A bee*
Un appareil nm | *A device*
Une bouteille nf | *A bottle*
Un conseil nm | *An advice*
Conseiller v | *To advise*
Une corbeille nf | *A trash can*
Une corneille nf | *A crow*
Une groseille nf | *A gooseberry*
Marseille nf | *Marseille*
Merveilleux – Merveilleuse adj | *Wonderful*

Une oreille nf | *An ear*
Un oreiller nm | *A pillow*
Un orteil nm | *A toe*
Pareil – Pareille adj | *Same*
Un réveil nm | *An alarm clock*
Se réveiller v | *To wake up*
Le soleil nm | *The sun*
Le sommeil nm | *Sleep*
Surveiller v | *To watch*
Vieux – Vieille – Vieil adj | *Old*

LA FÊTE D'ANNIVERSAIRE DE MON FILS

MY SON'S BIRTHDAY PARTY

19

1. **Écoutez l'audio** et **lisez l'histoire** en même temps.
   Listen to the audio and read the story at the same time.

La fête d'anniversaire de mon fils

Aujourd'hui, c'est l'anniversaire de mon fils. Il a sept ans. Tous ses amis arriveront dans quelques heures pour la fête qu'on a organisée. Je dois me dépêcher pour tout faire. Je vais d'abord aller chercher son gâteau que j'ai commandé à la boulangerie. J'ai oublié d'acheter des bougies donc je dois aller en acheter au magasin. Une fois rentrée, je dois accrocher les banderoles et mettre la table. Un château gonflable sera livré dans deux heures et installé dans le jardin. Je vais mettre deux tables près du château gonflable. La première avec des chips et de petites choses à grignoter et la deuxième avec des boissons. La dernière chose à faire après tout ça, c'est d'emballer ses cadeaux. Je devrais avoir assez de temps pour tout faire. J'espère juste que personne ne sera malade dans le château gonflable car il y a beaucoup à manger !

TRANSLATION

My Son's Birthday Party

Today is my son's birthday. He is seven years old. All his friends will arrive in a few hours for the party we threw. I have to hurry to get everything done. I'll first get his cake, which I ordered from the bakery. I forgot to buy candles, so I have to buy some at the store. Once I get home, I have to hang the banners and set the table. A bouncy castle will be delivered in two hours and set up in the garden. I'm going to put two tables near the bouncy castle. The first is for chips and small snacks, and the second is for drinks. The last thing to do after all this is to wrap his presents. I should have enough time to do everything. I hope no one gets sick in the bouncy castle because there's plenty to eat!

2. **Écoutez l'audio 19.1** et **numérotez les phrases de 1 à 13 pour les remettre dans l'ordre.**
   Listen to the audio 19.1 and number the sentences from 1 to 13 to put them in order.

– Je devrais avoir assez de temps pour tout faire.

– Je vais d'abord aller chercher son gâteau que j'ai commandé à la boulangerie.

– Aujourd'hui, c'est l'anniversaire de mon fils.

– La dernière chose à faire après tout ça, c'est d'emballer ses cadeaux.

– Je vais mettre deux tables près du château gonflable.

– Tous ses amis arriveront dans quelques heures pour la fête qu'on a organisée.

– J'espère juste que personne ne sera malade dans le château gonflable car il y a beaucoup à manger !

– Il a sept ans.

– Une fois rentrée, je dois accrocher les banderoles et mettre la table.

– La première avec des chips et de petites choses à grignoter et la deuxième avec des boissons.

– Un château gonflable sera livré dans deux heures et installé dans le jardin.

– Je dois me dépêcher pour tout faire.

– J'ai oublié d'acheter des bougies donc je dois aller en acheter au magasin.

AUDIO 19.2 🔊

VOCABULARY

Une fête d'anniversaire nf | *A birthday party*
Un fils nm | *A son*
Avoir ... ans v | *To be ... years*
Un ami – Une amie n | *A friend*
Arriver v | *To arrive*
Une heure nf | *An hour*
Organiser v | *To organize*
Se dépêcher v | *To hurry*
Chercher v | *To get – To pick up*
Un gâteau nm | *A cake*
Commander v | *To order*
Une boulangerie nf | *A bakery*
Acheter v | *To buy*
Une bougie nf | *A candle*
Un magasin nm | *A store*
Accrocher v | *To hang*

Une banderole nf | *A banner*
Une table nf | *A table*
Un château gonflable nm | *A bouncy castle*
Livrer v | *To deliver*
Installer v | *To set up*
Le jardin nm | *The garden*
La première nf | *The first*
Des chips nf | *Chips*
Une chose nf | *A thing*
Grignoter v | *To snack*
La deuxième nf | *The second*
Une boisson nf | *A drink*
Emballer v | *To wrap*
Un cadeau nm | *A gift*
Malade adj | *Sick*

UNE JOURNÉE AU ZOO
A DAY AT THE ZOO

What is a Liaison?

A liaison in French is when the final silent consonant of a word is pronounced because the following word begins with a vowel or a silent "h." This helps make the pronunciation of groups of words more fluid.

Here are the three different types of liaisons we will focus on in this exercise:

AUDIO 20.1 ◀))

The Z Sound

The **Z sound** happens when the final consonant is an **s** and the next word begins with a vowel or a silent h.

Les oranges = Les Zoranges
Oranges

The T Sound

The **T sound** happens when the final consonant is a **t** and the next word begins with a vowel or a silent h.

Ils font un gâteau. = Ils font Tun gâteau.
They are making a cake.

The N Sound

The **N sound** happens when the final consonant is a **n** and the next word begins with a vowel or a silent h.

Un avis = Un Navis
An opinion

AUDIO 20.2 ◀))

1. **Écoutez l'audio** et soulignez **les liaisons** comme dans les exemples ci-dessus.
   Listen to the audio and underline the liaisons like in the examples above.

Une journée au zoo

Nos enfants adorent aller au zoo. Ils aiment admirer les animaux. Ils peuvent passer des heures à regarder les éléphants et les ours. Ils sont toujours contents de les observer pendant qu'ils mangent, qu'ils dorment, ou qu'ils se promènent dans leurs enclos. Mais au zoo, il n'y a pas que les gros mammifères, il y a aussi les oiseaux, les reptiles et les poissons. Les cages des oiseaux sont immenses et les aquariums sont plein de couleurs vives. Avec tous les animaux qu'il y a à voir, une journée au zoo passe toujours trop vite. Les enfants ont toujours hâte d'y retourner.

TRANSLATION

A Day at the Zoo

Our children love going to the zoo. They like to admire the animals. They can spend hours watching elephants and bears. They are always happy to watch them while they eat, sleep, or walk around their enclosures. But at the zoo, there are not only large mammals, there are also birds, reptiles and fish. The bird cages are huge and the aquariums are full of bright colors. With all the animals there are to see, a day at the zoo always goes by too quickly. The children always look forward to going back.

AUDIO 20.3 ◀))
VOCABULARY

Une orange nf | *An orange*
Un gâteau nm | *A cake*
Un avis nm | *An opinion*
Une journée nf | *A day*
Le zoo nm | *The zoo*
Un – Une enfant n | *A child*
Adorer v | *To like*
Admirer v | *To admire*
Un animal – Des animaux nm |
An animal – Animals
Passer des heures | *To spend hours*
Regarder v | *To watch*
Un éléphant nm | *An elephant*
Un ours nm | *A bear*
Content – Contente adj | *Happy*
Observer v | *To watch*

Manger v | *To eat*
Dormir v | *To sleep*
Se promener v | *To walk*
Un enclos nm | *An enclosure*
Un gros mammifère adj + nm | *A big mammal*
Un oiseau nm | *A bird*
Un reptile nm | *A reptile*
Un poisson nm | *A fish*
Une cage nf | *A cage*
Immense adj | *Huge*
Un aquarium nm | *An aquarium*
Plein – Pleine adj | *Full*
Une couleur vive nf + adj | *A bright color*
Vite adv | *Quickly*
Retourner v | *To go back*

UN NOUVEAU CAMPING-CAR
A NEW MOTORHOME

21

AUDIO 21.1 ◄))

1. **Écoutez l'audio** et **lisez l'histoire** en même temps.
   Listen to the audio and read the story at the same time.

Un nouveau camping-car

J'adore faire du camping mais je déteste dormir en tente. Dormir sur un matelas gonflable, ce n'est jamais confortable. Sans parler des animaux qui vivent autour des campings. Cette année, on a décidé d'acheter un camping-car. Je pense que je me sentirais mieux si je dormais à l'intérieur au lieu de dans une tente. C'est cher mais on fait du camping au moins dix fois par an donc ça en vaut la peine. Cela fait un peu plus de trois mois qu'on regarde les petites annonces tous les jours, mais rien. Personne ne vend un camping-car au milieu de l'hiver. Maintenant que c'est le printemps, on voit de plus en plus d'annonces chaque jour mais ce n'est jamais ce qu'on cherche. Mais ce matin, tout a changé. Je prenais mon café en regardant les petites annonces sur mon ordinateur quand je l'ai vu ; le camping-car de nos rêves ! Il a seulement cinq ans et il a très peu de kilomètres au compteur. La personne qui le vend habite seulement à dix kilomètres de chez nous ! On va le voir cet après-midi mais je pense que c'est le bon. Le prix est parfait et j'ai hâte de ne plus dormir en tente.

TRANSLATION

A New Motorhome

I love camping, but I hate sleeping in a tent. Sleeping on an inflatable mattress is never comfortable. Not to mention the animals that live around the campsites. This year, we decided to buy a motorhome. I think I would feel better if I slept inside instead of in a tent. It's expensive, but we go camping at least ten times a year, so it's worth it. We've been looking at the classified ads every day for a little over three months, but nothing. No one sells a camper in the middle of winter. Now that it's spring, we see more and more ads every day, but it's never what we're looking for. This morning, everything changed. I was having my coffee while looking at the classifieds on my computer when I saw it: the motorhome of our dreams! It is only five years old and has very few kilometres on the odometer. The person who is selling it lives only ten kilometres from us! We're going to see it this afternoon, but I think it's the right one. The price is perfect, and I can't wait to no longer sleep in a tent.

Un nouveau camping-car

J'adore faire du camping mais je déteste _____ en tente. Dormir sur un _____ gonflable, ce n'est jamais confortable. Sans parler des _____ qui vivent autour des campings. Cette année, on a décidé d'acheter un camping-car. Je pense que je me sentirais mieux si je dormais à l'intérieur au lieu de dans une tente. C'est cher mais on fait du camping au moins dix _____ par an donc ça en vaut la peine. Cela fait un peu plus de trois _____ qu'on regarde les petites annonces tous les jours, mais _____. Personne ne vend un camping-car au milieu de l' _____. Maintenant que c'est le _____, on voit de plus en plus d'annonces chaque jour mais ce n'est jamais ce qu'on cherche. Mais ce matin, tout a changé. Je prenais mon _____ en regardant les petites annonces sur mon ordinateur quand je l'ai vu ; le camping-car de nos _____ ! Il a seulement cinq ans et il a très peu de _____ au compteur. La personne qui le vend habite seulement à dix kilomètres de chez nous ! On va le voir cet après-midi mais je pense que c'est le _____. Le prix est parfait et j'ai hâte de ne plus dormir en tente.

AUDIO 21.2 ◀))

VOCABULARY

Nouveau – Nouvelle adj | *New*
Un camping-car nm | *A motorhome*
Adorer v | *To love*
Faire du camping | *To camp*
Détester v | *To hate*
Dormir v | *To sleep*
Une tente nf | *A tent*
Un matelas gonflable nm | *An inflatable mattress*
Confortable adj | *Comfortable*
Un animal – Des animaux nm |
An animal – Animals
Vivre v | *To live*
Acheter v | *To buy*
Se sentir v | *To feel*
Cher – Chère adj | *Expensive*
Une fois nf | *One time*
En valoir la peine | *To be worth it*

Un mois nm | *A month*
Regarder v | *To look*
Les petites annonces nf | *The classified ads*
Vendre v | *To sell*
L'hiver nm | *Winter*
Le printemps nm | *Spring*
Chercher v | *To look for*
Prendre un café | *To have a coffee*
Un ordinateur nm | *A computer*
... de nos rêves | *... of our dream*
Un kilomètre nm | *A kilometre*
Un compteur nm | *An odometer*
Habiter v | *To live*
Un après-midi nm | *An afternoon*
Le prix nm | *The price*
Parfait – Parfaite adj | *Perfect*

LE SON AILLE
THE SOUND AILLE

22

The sound **aille** has two possible spellings in French. It's spelled **ail** and **aille**.

AUDIO 22.1 🔊

ail   **Le trav<u>ail</u>** nm | *Work*
aill(e)   **Une bat<u>aille</u>** nf | *A battle*

When the sound **aille** is at the end of a noun, masculine nouns end in **ail**, feminine nouns end in **aille**.

This exercise, "Listen and repeat," is divided into four different parts:

1. The sound only
2. The sound in syllables
3. The sound in words
4. Write down the words you hear

AUDIO 22.2 🔊

1. Écoutez **le son aille** et répétez après moi.
   *Listen to the sound **aille** and repeat after me.*

→ *A good way to explain this sound is to pronounce **a** + the beginning of **"yes"** in English.*
*I like to explain as **a + a rolling y**.*

ail – aille

AUDIO 22.3 🔊

2. Écoutez **le son aille** dans **les différentes syllabes** et répétez après moi.
   *Listen to the sound **aille** in the different syllables and repeat after me.*

**baille – caille – daille – faille – jaille – laille – maille – naille – paille – raille –
saille – taille – vaille – zaille**

3. Écoutez **les différents mots** incluant le son **aille** et répétez après moi.
   *Listen to the different words including the sound **aille** and repeat after me.*

Un b<u>ail</u>

Un c<u>aill</u>ou

Un chand<u>ail</u>

Un évent<u>ail</u>

Une m<u>aille</u>

Un p<u>aill</u>asson

Un port<u>ail</u>

Un t<u>aille</u>-crayon

Une trouv<u>aille</u>

Un vitr<u>ail</u>

4. Écrivez **les mots** que vous entendez. Si vous ne comprenez pas le mot complet,
   écrivez une ou deux syllabes.
   *Write down the words you hear. If you don't understand the full word, write one or
   two syllables.*

1. L'

2. Une

3. Un

4. Un

5. Un

6. Une

7. Une

8. Le

9.

10.

VOCABULARY

L'ail nm | *Garlic*

Un bail nm | *A lease*

Une bataille nf | *A battle*

Un caillou nm | *A rock*

Un chandail nm | *A sweater*

Un détail nm | *A detail*

Un épouvantail nm | *A scarecrow*

Un éventail nm | *A fan*

Une maille nf | *A stitch*

Un maillot nm | *A swimsuit*

Une médaille nf | *A medal*

Un paillasson nm | *A doormat*

Une paille nf | *A straw*

Un portail nm | *An entrance*

Le rail nm | *Rail*

Un taille-crayon nm | *A pencil sharpener*

Tailler v | *To prune*

Travailler v | *To work*

Une trouvaille nf | *A discovery*

Un vitrail nm | *Stained glass*

UNE MACHINE À PAIN
A BREAD MACHINE

23

AUDIO 23.1 ◀》

1. **Écoutez l'audio** et **lisez l'histoire** en même temps.
   Listen to the audio and read the story at the same time.

Une machine à pain

On vient d'acheter une machine à pain et je n'arrive pas à croire qu'on n'en ait pas acheté une avant ! La machine fait tout pour nous. La seule chose qu'on doit faire, c'est d'y mettre tous les ingrédients. On commence par l'eau, puis la farine et le sel, avant d'ajouter la levure en dernier. On choisit les options et la machine pétrit le pain et le cuit en quelques heures. Avant ça, on faisait notre pain à la main et c'était toujours beaucoup de travail. Il fallait mélanger les ingrédients et puis pétrir la pâte pendant une dizaine de minutes. La pâte devait reposer pendant deux heures. Une fois bien levée, il fallait la pétrir de nouveau. En plus du travail, c'était aussi très salissant. Il y avait toujours de la farine partout et de la pâte collée sur le plan de travail. Je ne ferai plus jamais mon pain à la main maintenant que j'ai une machine à pain !

TRANSLATION

A Bread Machine

We just bought a bread machine, and I can't believe we didn't buy one before! The machine does everything for us. The only thing we have to do is add all the ingredients. We start with water, then flour and salt, before adding the yeast last. You choose the options, and the machine kneads the bread and bakes it in a few hours. Before that, we made our bread by hand, and it was always a lot of work. You had to mix the ingredients and then knead the dough for around ten minutes. The dough had to rest for two hours. Once risen, it had to be kneaded again. In addition to work, it was also very messy. There was always flour everywhere and dough stuck to the countertop. I will never make my bread by hand again now that I have a bread machine!

2. **Écoutez l'audio 23.1** et **numérotez les phrases de 1 à 12 pour les remettre dans l'ordre.**
   Listen to the audio 23.1 and number the sentences from 1 to 12 to put them in order.

   – On choisit les options et la machine pétrit le pain et le cuit en quelques heures.

   – Une fois bien levée, il fallait la pétrir de nouveau.

– En plus du travail, c'était aussi très salissant.

– La seule chose qu'on doit faire, c'est d'y mettre tous les ingrédients.

– Je ne ferai plus jamais mon pain à la main maintenant que j'ai une machine à pain !

– On commence par l'eau, puis la farine et le sel, avant d'ajouter la levure en dernier.

– Il fallait mélanger les ingrédients et puis pétrir la pâte pendant une dizaine de minutes.

– La machine fait tout pour nous.

– Avant ça, on faisait notre pain à la main et c'était toujours beaucoup de travail.

– La pâte devait reposer pendant deux heures.

– On vient d'acheter une machine à pain et je n'arrive pas à croire qu'on n'en ait pas acheté une avant !

– Il y avait toujours de la farine partout et de la pâte collée sur le plan de travail.

AUDIO 23.2 ◄))

VOCABULARY

Une machine à pain nf | *A bread machine*
Acheter v | *To buy*
Croire v | *To believe*
Avant adv | *Before*
Tout adj | *Everything*
La seule chose adj + nf | *The only thing*
Mettre v | *To add*
Un ingrédient nm | *An ingredient*
De l'eau nf | *Water*
De la farine nf | *Flour*
Du sel nm | *Salt*
Ajouter v | *To add*
De la levure nf | *Yeast*
Choisir v | *To choose*
Une option nf | *An option*
Pétrir v | *To knead*

Un pain nm | *A loaf of bread*
Cuire v | *To bake*
À la main adv | *By hand*
Du travail nm | *Work*
Mélanger v | *To mix*
La pâte nf | *The dough*
Une dizaine de minutes | *About ten minutes*
Reposer v | *To rest*
Levé – Levée pp | *Risen*
De nouveau adv | *Again*
Salissant – Salissante adj | *Messy*
Partout adv | *Eveywhere*
Collé – Collée pp | *Stuck*
Un plan de travail nm | *A countertop*
Jamais adv | *Never*

LE MARCHÉ DE NOËL
THE CHRISTMAS MARKET

24

What is a Liaison?

A liaison in French is when the final silent consonant of a word is pronounced because the following word begins with a vowel or a silent "h." This helps make the pronunciation of groups of words more fluid.

Here are the three different types of liaisons we will focus on in this exercise:

AUDIO 24.1 ◀))

The Z Sound

The **Z sound** happens when the final consonant is an **s** and the next word begins with a vowel or a silent h.

Les idées = Le_s Zidées
Ideas

The T Sound

The **T sound** happens when the final consonant is a **t** and the next word begins with a vowel or a silent h.

C'est une surprise. = C'es_t Tune surprise.
It's a surprise.

The N Sound

The **N sound** happens when the final consonant is a **n** and the next word begins with a vowel or a silent h.

Un avocat = U_n Navocat
An avocado

AUDIO 24.2 ◀))

1. **Écoutez l'audio** et soulignez **les liaisons** comme dans les exemples ci-dessus.
   Listen to the audio and underline the liaisons like in the examples above.

Le marché de Noël

Tous les ans, la ville organise un incroyable marché de Noël au mois de décembre. Il ouvre ses portes le 1er décembre. Les visiteurs viennent de toute la France pour faire des achats, déguster du vin chaud, et s'imprégner de l'ambiance de Noël. Beaucoup de vendeurs sont des artistes.

Ils fabriquent eux-mêmes les décorations, les jouets et les produits artisanaux qu'ils vendent. Les enfants, eux, sont là pour les chocolats chauds et le sapin géant au milieu du marché. Les odeurs de vin chaud et de pain d'épices, ainsi que les musiques de Noël remplissent les rues de la ville. Chaque année, c'est un succès pour les petits et les grands.

TRANSLATION

The Christmas Market

Every year, the city organizes an incredible Christmas market in December. It opens its doors on December 1st. Visitors come from all over France to shop, enjoy mulled wine, and soak up the Christmas spirit. Many sellers are artists. They make the decorations, toys and crafts they sell themselves. The children are there for the hot chocolates and the giant Christmas tree in the middle of the market. The smells of mulled wine and gingerbread, as well as Christmas music, fill the city streets. Every year, it's a success for young and old.

AUDIO 24.3 ◀))

VOCABULARY

Une idée nf | *An idea*
Une surprise nf | *A surprise*
Un avocat nm | *An avocado*
La ville nf | *The city*
Organiser v | *To organize*
Incroyable adj | *Incredible*
Un marché de Noël nm | *A Christmas Market*
Décembre nm | *December*
Ouvrir ses portes | *To open its doors*
Un visiteur – Une visiteuse n | *A visitor*
La France nf | *France*
Un achat nm | *A purchase*
Déguster v | *To enjoy*
Du vin chaud nm | *Mulled wine*
S'imprégner v | *To soak up*

L'ambiance de Noël nf | *Christmas spirit*
Un – Une artiste n | *An artist*
Fabriquer v | *To make*
Une décoration nf | *A decoration*
Un jouet nm | *A toy*
Un produit artisanal nm + adj | *Craft*
Un – Une enfant n | *A child*
Un chocolat chaud nm + adj | *Hot chocolate*
Un sapin géant nm + adj | *A giant tree*
Une odeur nf | *A smell*
Un pain d'épices nm | *A gingerbread*
Une musique de Noël nf | *Christmas music*
Remplir v | *To fill*
Un succès nm | *A success*
Les petits et les grands | *Young and old*

QUEL MOT EST-CE QUE JE PRONONCE ?
WHAT WORD DO I PRONOUNCE?

25

AUDIO 25.1 ◀))

Écoutez **l'audio** et **entourez** le mot que je prononce. Chaque mot est répété deux fois.
La liste des mots est traduite après cet exercice.
Listen to the audio and circle the word I say. Each word is repeated twice. The list of words is translated after this exercise.

1. Surpris – Surprise
2. Jaune – Jeune
3. Café – Carré
4. Cabane – Cabine
5. Balle – Boule
6. Pousser – Passer
7. Rouge – Rage

8. Goût – Goutte
9. Rêve – Rive
10. Lieu – Vieux
11. Talon – Talent
12. Roman – Romain
13. Lever – Laver
14. Payer – Pays

15. Vue – Vie
16. Banc – Bon
17. Prendre – Pendre
18. Feu – Fou
19. Prêt – Prête
20. Casier – Caissier

AUDIO 25.2 ◀))

VOCABULARY

Surpris – Surprise adj | *Surprised*
Une surprise nf | *A surprise*
Jaune adj | *Yellow*
Jeune adj | *Young*
Un café nm | *A coffee*
Un carré nm | *A square*
Une cabane nf | *A shed*
Une cabine nf | *A changing room*
Une balle nf | *A ball*
Une boule nf | *A ball*
Pousser v | *To push*
Passer v | *To pass*
Rouge adj | *Red*
La rage nf | *Rabies*
Le goût nm | *Taste*
Une goutte nf | *A drop*
Un rêve nm | *A dream*
Une rive nf | *A shore*
Un lieu nm | *A place*
Vieux – Vieille adj | *Old*

Un talon nm | *A heel*
Un talent nm | *A talent*
Un roman nm | *A novel*
Un romain nm | *A Roman*
Lever v | *To lift*
Laver v | *To wash*
Payer v | *To pay*
Un pays nm | *A country*
La vue nf | *The view*
La vie nf | *Life*
Un banc nm | *A bench*
Bon – Bonne adj | *Good*
Prendre v | *To take*
Pendre v | *To hung*
Un feu nm | *A fire*
Fou – Folle adj | *Crazy*
Prêt – Prête adj | *Ready*
Un casier nm | *A locker*
Un caissier – Une caissière n | *A cashier*

LA LETTRE MUETTE T
THE SILENT LETTER T

26

What is a Silent Letter?

A silent letter in French is a letter that is not pronounced. A silent letter is usually at the end of a word.

T is a common silent letter in French but not as common as **e** or **s**.

Here are the two types of words where you can find the silent letter **t** in French:

AUDIO 26.1 ◄))

At the end of nouns, adjectives and adverbs

Un lit nm | *A bed*
Un achat nm | *A purchase*

Inquiet adj | *Worried*
Absent adj | *Absent*

Lentement adv | *Slowly*
Calmement adv | *Calmly*

AUDIO 26.2 ◄))

When a verb is conjugated with il – elle – on – ils – elles

Il dit v | *He is saying*
Il vient v | *He comes*

Elle lit v | *She is reading*
Elle tient v | *She is holding*

On interdit v | *We forgive*
On devient v | *We become*

Ils mangent v | *They are eating*
Ils dorment v | *They are sleeping*

Elles parlent v | *They are speaking*
Elles chantent v | *They are singing*

Note that the verb **être** conjugated in the present tense "**Il est** – *He is*" doesn't contain a silent **t**; **est** makes the sound **è** and is not considered a silent letter.

1. Écoutez la différence lorsque **la lettre t** est **prononcée** et **non prononcée**.
   *Listen to the difference when the letter **t** is pronounced and not pronounced.*

   Un but – *A goal*
   Un lit – *A bed*

2. Écoutez ces 20 phrases et **entourez les mots** où **la lettre t est muette**.
   *Listen to these 20 sentences and circle the words where the letter **t** is silent.*

1. Elles n'aiment pas le chocolat blanc.

2. C'est un objet bizarre.

3. Il a beaucoup de talent.

4. Le professeur sera absent ce vendredi.

5. Mon mari est un homme galant.

6. Le chat dort devant le feu ouvert.

7. Il y a eu un accident près de chez moi la nuit dernière.

8. Les Français mangent des escargots.

9. Il ne fait jamais attention à ses affaires.

10. Ce bâtiment va être démoli au mois de juillet.

11. Notre séjour était parfait !

12. Mes parents se reposent dans le salon.

13. Il y a beaucoup d'accents sur les lettres en français.

14. Est-ce que tu es prêt ?

15. Notre chien est plus petit que le tien.

16. Tu veux aller au restaurant avant ou après le cinéma ?

17. Le résultat des élections sera connu demain.

18. J'aurai fini le rapport demain.

19. Les habitants du village organisent un marché de Noël chaque année.

20. Il faut se concentrer sur le présent.

TRANSLATION

1. *They don't like white chocolate.*

2. *It's a weird object.*

3. *He has a lot of talent.*

4. *The teacher will be absent this Friday.*

5. *My husband is a gallant man.*

6. *The cat sleeps in front of the open fire.*

7. *There was an accident near my house last night.*

8. *The French eat snails.*

9. *He never pays attention to his stuffs.*

10. *This building will be demolished in July.*

11. *Our stay was perfect!*

12. *My parents are resting in the living room.*

13. *There are a lot of accents on letters in French.*

14. *Are you ready?*

15. *Our dog is smaller than yours.*

16. *Do you want to go to a restaurant before or after the cinema?*

17. *The election results will be known tomorrow.*

18. *I will have finished the report tomorrow.*

19. *The residents of the village organize a Christmas market every year.*

20. *You have to focus on the present.*

VOCABULARY

Un lit nm | *A bed*
Un achat nm | *A purchase*
Inquiet adj | *Worried*
Absent adj | *Absent*
Lentement adv | *Slowly*
Calmement adv | *Calmly*
Il dit (Dire) v | *He is saying (To say)*
Il vient (Venir) v | *He comes (To come)*
Elle lit (Lire) v | *She is reading (To read)*
Elle tient (Tenir) v | *She is holding (To hold)*
On interdit (Interdire) v | *We forgive (To forgive)*
On devient (Devenir) v | *We become (To become)*
Ils mangent (Manger) v | *They are eating (To eat)*

Ils dorment (Dormir) v | *They are sleeping (To sleep)*
Elles parlent (Parler) v | *They are speaking (To speak)*
Elles chantent (Chanter) v | *They are singing (To sing)*
Un but nm | *A goal*
Aimer v | *To like*
Du chocolat blanc nm | *White chocolate*
Un objet nm | *An object*
Bizarre adj | *Weird*
Du talent nm | *Talent*
Un professeur nm | *A teacher*
Le vendredi nm | *Friday*
Un mari nm | *A husband*
Un homme nm | *A man*

Galant adj | *Gallant*

Un chat nm | *A cat*

Dormir v | *To sleep*

Devant adv | *In front of*

Un feu ouvert nm | *An open fire*

Un accident nm | *An accident*

La nuit dernière nf + adj | *Last night*

Un Français – Une Française n |
A French person

Manger v | *To eat*

Un escargot nm | *A snail*

Des affaires nf | *Stuffs*

Un bâtiment nm | *A building*

Démolir v | *To demolish*

Un mois nm | *A month*

Juillet nm | *July*

Un séjour nm | *A stay*

Parfait adj | *Perfect*

Des parents nm | *Parents*

Se reposer v | *To rest*

Un salon nm | *A living room*

Un accent nm | *An accent*

Une lettre nf | *A letter*

Le français nm | *French*

Prêt adj | *Ready*

Un chien nm | *A dog*

Petit adj | *Small*

Un restaurant nm | *A restaurant*

Avant adv | *Before*

Après adv | *After*

Un cinéma nm | *A cinema*

Le résultat nm | *The result*

Une élection nf | *An election*

Un rapport nm | *A report*

Un habitant – Une habitante n | *A resident*

Un village nm | *A village*

Organiser v | *To organize*

Un marché de Noël nm | *A Christmas market*

Se concentrer v | *To focus*

Le présent nm | *The present*

QU'EST-CE QUE J'AI DANS MON SAC ?
WHAT DO I HAVE IN MY PURSE?

27

AUDIO 27.1 ◄))

1. **Écoutez l'audio** et **lisez l'histoire** en même temps.
   Listen to the audio and read the story at the same time.

Qu'est-ce que j'ai dans mon sac ?

J'ai beaucoup de choses dans mon sac, beaucoup trop de choses je pense. J'ai mon portefeuille avec mes documents d'identités et mes cartes bancaires. J'ai les clés de mon appartement, de ma voiture et les clés de mon bureau. J'ai mon téléphone bien sûr, parfois j'ai aussi son chargeur si je n'ai plus de batterie. J'ai quelques produits de beauté comme du beurre de cacao et de la crème pour les mains ainsi qu'une petite bouteille de désinfectant pour les mains. Ça, c'est l'essentiel. Pour le reste, j'ai aussi un stylo, un petit cahier, un paquet de mouchoirs et un sac réutilisable pour faire mes courses. Le plus compliqué, c'est quand je change de sac. Je dois tout vider et décider ce que je garde ou pas.

TRANSLATION

What Do I Have in my Purse?

I have a lot of things in my purse, way too many things I think. I have my wallet with my ID and my bank cards. I have the keys to my apartment, car, and office. I have my phone, of course; sometimes I also have its charger if I'm out of battery. I have a few beauty products like cocoa butter, hand cream, and a small bottle of hand sanitizer. These are the main things. For the rest, I also have a pen, a small notebook, a pack of tissues and a reusable bag for shopping. The most complicated thing is when I change purses. I have to empty everything and decide what to keep and what not to keep.

2. **Écoutez l'audio 27.1** et ajoutez **les mots manquants**.
   Listen to the audio 27.1 and add the missing words.

Qu'est-ce que j'ai dans mon sac ?

J'ai beaucoup de _____ dans mon sac, beaucoup trop de choses je _____ . J'ai mon portefeuille avec mes _____ d'identités et mes cartes bancaires. J'ai les clés de mon appartement, de ma _____ et les clés de mon bureau. J'ai mon _____ bien sûr, parfois j'ai aussi son chargeur si je n'ai plus de   . J'ai quelques produits de beauté comme du beurre

de cacao et de la   pour les mains ainsi qu'une petite bouteille de

désinfectant pour les mains. Ça, c'est l'essentiel. Pour le   , j'ai aussi

un stylo, un petit cahier, un   de mouchoirs et un sac réutilisable pour

faire mes   . Le plus compliqué, c'est quand je

de sac. Je dois tout vider et décider ce que je   ou pas.

AUDIO 27.2 ◄))

VOCABULARY

Un sac nm | *A purse*
Une chose nf | *A thing*
Penser v | *To think*
Un portefeuille nm | *A wallet*
Des documents d'identités nm |
Identity documents/ID
Une carte bancaire nf | *A bank card*
Une clé nf | *A key*
Un appartement nm | *An apartment*
Une voiture nf | *A car*
Un bureau nm | *An office*
Un téléphone nm | *A phone*
Un chargeur nm | *A charger*
De la batterie nf | *Battery*
Un produit de beauté nm | *A beauty product*
Du beurre de cacao nm | *Cocoa butter*

De la crème pour les mains nf | *Hand cream*
Une petite bouteille adj + nf | *A little bottle*
Du désinfectant nm | *Hand sanitizer*
L'essentiel nm | *The essential*
Le reste nm | *The rest*
Un stylo nm | *A pen*
Un petit cahier adj + nm | *A small notebook*
Un paquet de mouchoirs nm | *A pack of tissues*
Un sac réutilisable nm + adj | *A reusable bag*
Faire les courses | *To shop*
Compliqué – Compliquée adj | *Complicated*
Changer v | *To change*
Vider v | *To empty*
Décider v | *To decide*
Garder v | *To keep*

LE SON ILLE
THE SOUND ILLE

28

The sound **ille** has only one spelling and it's **ille**. Note that the spelling ille is sometimes pronounced as **i** followed by **l**, such as "**Une ville** – *A city*" or "**Mille** – *One hundred*."

AUDIO 28.1 ◀))

ill(e)   **La vanille** nf | *Vanilla*

This exercise, "Listen and repeat," is divided into four different parts:

1.   The sound only
2.   The sound in syllables
3.   The sound in words
4.   Write down the words you hear

AUDIO 28.2 ◀))

1. Écoutez **le son ille** et répétez après moi.
   *Listen to the sound **ille** and repeat after me.*

   ille

AUDIO 28.3 ◀))

2. Écoutez **le son ille** dans **les différentes syllabes** et répétez après moi.
   *Listen to the sound **ille** in the different syllables and repeat after me.*

   bille – cille – dille – fille – jille – lille – mille – nille – pille – rille – sille –
   tille – ville – zille

AUDIO 28.4 ◀))

3. Écoutez **les différents mots** incluant le son **ille** et répétez après moi.
   *Listen to the different words including the sound **ille** and repeat after me.*

   Une bille
   Camille
   La camomille
   Une cheville
   Une cuillère

   Gaspiller
   Une jonquille
   Une lentille
   Un papillon
   S'habiller

4. Écrivez **les mots** que vous entendez. Si vous ne comprenez pas le mot complet, écrivez une ou deux syllabes.
Write down the words you hear. If you don't understand the full word, write one or two syllables.

1.

2. Une

3. Une

4. La

5. Une

6.

7. Une

8.

9. Une

10. La

VOCABULARY

Une bille nf | *A ball*
Briller v | *To shine*
Camille nf | *Camille*
La camomille nf | *Chamomille*
Une chenille nf | *A caterpillar*
Une cheville nf | *An ankle*
Une coquille nf | *A shell*
Une cuillère nf | *A spoon*
La famille nf | *Family*
Une fille nf | *A daughter*

Gaspiller v | *To waste*
Gentille adj | *Kind*
Une grille nf | *A grid*
Griller v | *To grill*
Une jonquille nf | *A dafodill*
Une lentille nf | *A lens*
Un papillon nm | *A butterfly*
Une quille nf | *A bowling pin*
S'habiller v | *To get dressed*
La vanille nf | *Vanilla*

MA PREMIÈRE TASSE DE CAFÉ

MY FIRST CUP OF COFFEE

29

AUDIO 29.1 ◀))

> 1. **Écoutez l'audio** et **lisez l'histoire** en même temps.
> *Listen to the audio and read the story at the same time.*

Ma première tasse de café

Je ne me souviens pas exactement de la première fois que j'ai goûté du café mais mes parents en préparaient une cruche tous les matins. Le plus souvent, c'était mon père qui remplissant la machine et y ajoutait du café moulu. Cela sentait toujours bon le café quand je me levais. Quand j'avais plus ou moins dix ans, je buvais quelques gorgées ici et là. Je ne trouvais pas ça très bon mais je voulais faire comme tout le monde. La première fois que j'ai bu une tasse de café complète, c'était au camping avec mon père. Il faisait froid et mon père avait oublié d'apporter du chocolat chaud. Pour me réchauffer, il m'a donné une tasse de café avec beaucoup de crème et de sucre. Je me souviens que cela m'a réchauffé immédiatement. Maintenant que je suis plus âgé, je bois une ou deux tasses de café le matin mais je le bois toujours noir, sans sucre et sans crème.

TRANSLATION

My First Cup of Coffee

I don't remember exactly the first time that I tasted coffee, but my parents made a pot of it every morning. Most often, my father filled the machine and added ground coffee. It always smelled like coffee when I got up. When I was about ten years old, I had a few sips here and there. I didn't think it was very good, but I wanted to do it like everyone else. The first time I drank a full cup of coffee was camping with my dad. It was cold, and my father had forgotten to bring hot chocolate. He gave me a cup of coffee with lots of cream and sugar to warm me up. I remember it warmed me up immediately. Now that I'm older, I drink one or two cups of coffee in the morning, but I always drink it black, without sugar and cream.

> 2. **Écoutez l'audio 29.1** et **numérotez les phrases de 1 à 10 pour les remettre dans l'ordre.**
> *Listen to the audio 29.1 and number the sentences from 1 to 10 to put them in order.*

— Je ne trouvais pas ça très bon mais je voulais faire comme tout le monde.

— Le plus souvent, c'était mon père qui remplissant la machine et y ajoutait du café moulu.

– Quand j'avais plus ou moins dix ans, je buvais quelques gorgées ici et là.

– Je ne me souviens pas exactement de la première fois que j'ai goûté du café mais mes parents en préparaient une cruche tous les matins.

– Pour me réchauffer, il m'a donné une tasse de café avec beaucoup de crème et de sucre.

– La première fois que j'ai bu une tasse de café complète, c'était au camping avec mon père.

– Je me souviens que cela m'a réchauffé immédiatement.

– Il faisait froid et mon père avait oublié d'apporter du chocolat chaud.

– Maintenant que je suis plus âgé, je bois une ou deux tasses de café le matin mais je le bois toujours noir, sans sucre et sans crème.

– Cela sentait toujours bon le café quand je me levais.

AUDIO 29.2 ◄))

VOCABULARY

Premier – Première adj | *First*
Une tasse de café nf | *A cup of coffee*
Se souvenir v | *To remember*
La première fois adj + nf | *The first time*
Goûter v | *To taste*
Du café nm | *Coffee*
Les parents nm | *The parents*
Préparer v | *To make*
Une cruche nf | *A pot*
Tous les matins adv | *Every morning*
Le père nm | *The father*
Remplir v | *To fill*
Une machine nf | *A machine*
Du café moulu nm + adj | *Ground coffee*
Sentir v | *To smell*
Se lever v | *To get up*
Boire v | *To drink*

Une gorgée nf | *A sip*
Trouver v | *To find*
Tout le monde adv | *Everyone else*
Complet – Complète adj | *Full*
Le camping nm | *Camping*
Faire froid v | *To be cold*
Oublier v | *To forget*
Apporter v | *To bring*
Du chocolat chaud nm | *Hot chocolate*
Réchauffer v | *To warm up*
De la crème nf | *Cream*
Du sucre nm | *Sugar*
Âgé – Âgée adj | *Older*
Le matin nm | *The morning*
Noir – Noire adj | *Black*
Sans adv | *Without*

BIENTÔT À LA RETRAITE
SOON TO RETIRE

30

AUDIO 30.1 ◀》

1. **Écoutez l'audio** et **lisez l'histoire** en même temps.
   Listen to the audio and read the story at the same time.

Bientôt à la retraite

Camille – J'ai appris que tu partais à la retraite à la fin du mois. Je ne savais pas ! Tu dois être ravi !

Steve – Oui, il était temps. Je voulais déjà prendre ma retraite l'année dernière mais mon patron m'a demandé de rester une année de plus.

Camille – Ah bon ? Pourquoi est-ce qu'il t'a demandé de rester ?

Steve – Parce que j'étais responsable d'un gros projet et c'était plus simple si je restais pour le finir. J'ai été bien payé pendant cette année et mes horaires étaient plus flexibles. Mais maintenant je suis prêt à me reposer et à voyager. Et toi ? Tu es à la retraite depuis un ou deux ans, non ?

Camille – Oui, je suis à la retraite depuis bientôt deux ans. Moi, en revanche, j'ai pris ma retraite une année plus tôt. Mon mari était déjà retraité et il voulait voyager plus donc j'ai décidé d'arrêter de travailler plus tôt.

Steve – Et tu es contente d'avoir arrêté plus tôt ?

Camille – Oui, cela nous a permis de voyager plus et de commencer la rénovation de notre maison. La seule chose qui est dommage, c'est que je ne touche pas ma retraite complète.

Steve – Il y a des pours et des contres partout. C'était chouette de te voir mais je dois y aller. J'ai une réunion.

Camille – Pas de problème. Ça m'a fait plaisir de te voir. À bientôt !

Steve – À bientôt !

TRANSLATION

Soon to Retire

Dylane – *I heard that you are retiring at the end of the month. I didn't know! You must be delighted!*

Steve – *Yes, it's about time. I already wanted to retire last year, but my boss asked me to stay for another year.*

Dylane – *Oh really? Why did he ask you to stay?*

Steve	–	Because I was responsible for a big project and it was easier if I stayed to finish it. I was paid well during this year and my hours were more flexible. But now I'm ready to rest and travel. And you? You've been retired for a year or two, right?
Dylane	–	Yes, I have been retired for almost two years. I, on the other hand, retired a year early. My husband was already retired, and he wanted to travel more, so I decided to stop working early.
Steve	–	And you're glad you stopped early?
Dylane	–	Yes, it allowed us to travel more and start renovating our house. The only thing that's too bad is that I don't receive my full pension.
Steve	–	There are pros and cons everywhere. It was nice seeing you, but I have to go. I have a meeting.
Dylane	–	No problem. It was nice to see you. See you soon!
Steve	–	See you soon!

2. **Écoutez l'audio une nouvelle fois** et ajoutez **le nom de la personne** à côté des faits listés. *Listen to the audio again and add the person's name next to the facts listed.*

1. Qui part à la retraite à la fin du mois ?
   Who will retire at the end of the month?

2. Qui est déjà à la retraite depuis bientôt deux ans ?
   Who has already been retired for almost two years?

3. Qui était responsable d'un gros projet ?
   Who was responsible for a big project?

4. Qui avait un mari déjà à la retraite ?
   Who had a husband who was already retired?

5. Qui a des horaires plus flexibles ?
   Who has more flexible hours?

6. Qui rénove sa maison ?
   Who is renovating their house?

7. Qui veut voyager ?
   Who wants to travel?

8. Qui ne touche pas sa pension complète ?
   Who doesn't get their full pension?

9. Qui a une réunion ?
   Who is having a meeting?

VOCABULARY

Bientôt adv | *Soon*
La retraite nf | *Retirement*
Apprendre v | *To learn*
Partir à la retraite | *To retire*
La fin du mois nf | *The end of the month*
Ravi – Ravie adj | *Delighted*
Prendre sa retraite | *To retire*
L'année dernière nf + adj | *Last year*
Un patron nm | *A boss*
Demander v | *To ask*
Rester v | *To stay*
Une année nf | *A year*
Responsable adj | *Responsible*
Un gros projet adj + nm | *A big project*
Simple adj | *Simple*
Finir v | *To finish*
Bien payé – payée adv + adj | *Well paid*
Les horaires nm | *Hours*
Flexible adj | *Flexible*

Prêt – Prête adj | *Ready*
Se reposer v | *To rest*
Voyager v | *To travel*
En revanche | *On the other hand*
Travailler v | *To work*
Tôt adv | *Early*
Content – Contente adj | *Happy*
Permettre v | *To allow*
Une rénovation nf | *A renovation*
Une maison nf | *A house*
C'est dommage | *That's too bad*
Toucher v | *To get (for money)*
Complet – Complète adj | *Full*
Des pours et des contres | *Pros and cons*
Chouette adj | *Nice*
Voir v | *To see*
Une réunion nf | *A meeting*
Pas de problème | *No problem*

LES COUPURES DE COURANT

POWER OUTAGES

31

1. **Écoutez l'audio** et **lisez l'histoire** en même temps.
   Listen to the audio and read the story at the same time.

Les coupures de courant

La météo où j'habite peut être un peu difficile. Ce n'est pas seulement où j'habite, c'est dans toute la région. On a toujours beaucoup de vent, surtout en automne. Le vent peut aller jusqu'à 100 km/h. C'est souvent le sujet de conversation préféré au magasin ou au café. À cause du vent, on a beaucoup de coupures de courant. Ce n'est pas très grave mais c'est toujours embêtant si on n'est pas préparé. On fait toujours attention à la météo mais parfois le vent semble arriver de nulle part. J'ai acheté une grosse batterie portable pour charger nos téléphones ou nos ordinateurs portables. Quand une coupure de courant dure plus d'une journée, il faut utiliser un générateur pour ne pas perdre toute la nourriture dans le frigo et le congélateur. Ce n'est pas la fin du monde mais il faut toujours être préparé.

TRANSLATION

Power Outages

The weather where I live can be difficult. It's not just where I live, it's throughout the region. We always have a lot of wind, especially in fall. The wind can reach up to 100 km/h. It's often the favorite topic of conversation at the store or cafe. Because of the wind, we have a lot of power outages. It's not very serious, but it's always annoying if you're unprepared. We always pay attention to the weather, but sometimes the wind seems to come out of nowhere. I bought a large portable battery to charge our phones and laptops. When a power outage lasts more than a day, you should use a generator so as not to lose all the food in the fridge and freezer. It's not the end of the world, but you always have to be prepared.

Les coupures de courant

La météo où j'habite peut être un peu   . Ce n'est pas seulement où j'habite, c'est dans toute la   . On a toujours beaucoup de vent, surtout en   . Le vent peut aller jusqu'à 100 km/h. C'est souvent le sujet de   préféré au magasin ou au   . À cause du vent, on a beaucoup de coupures de courant. Ce n'est pas très   mais c'est toujours embêtant si on n'est pas   . On fait toujours attention à la météo mais parfois le   semble arriver de nulle part. J'ai acheté une grosse   portable pour charger nos téléphones ou nos portables. Quand une coupure de courant dure plus d'une journée, il faut utiliser un générateur pour ne pas perdre toute la   dans le frigo et le congélateur. Ce n'est pas la fin du   mais il faut toujours être préparé.

AUDIO 31.2 ◀))

VOCABULARY

Une coupure de courant nf | *A power outage*
La météo nf | *The weather*
Habiter v | *To live*
Difficile adj | *Difficult*
Une région nf | *A region*
Du vent nm | *Wind*
L'automne nm | *Fall*
km/h – kilomètre heure |
km/h – kilometre hour
Un sujet de conversation nm |
A topic of conversation
Un magasin nm | *A store*
Un café nm | *A cafe*
Grave adj | *Serious*
Embêtant – Embêtante adj | *Annoying*
Être préparé – préparée v | *To be prepared*

Faire attention v | *To pay attention*
Sembler v | *To seem*
Nulle part adv | *Nowhere*
Une batterie portable nf | *A large battery*
Charger v | *To charge*
Un téléphone nm | *A phone*
Un ordinateur portable nm | *A laptop*
Durer v | *To last*
Une journée nf | *A day*
Un générateur nm | *A generator*
Perdre v | *To lose*
De la nourriture nf | *Food*
Un frigo nm | *A fridge*
Un congélateur nm | *A freezer*
La fin du monde nf | *The end of the world*

LE SON OUILLE
THE SOUND OUILLE

32

The sound **ouille** has two possible spellings in French: **ouil** and **ouille**. The most common is **ouille**.

ouil
ouill(e)

Du fenouil nm | *Fennel*
Fouiller v | *To rummage*

When the sound **ouille** is at the end of a noun, masculine nouns end in **ouil**, feminine nouns end in **ouille**.

This exercise, "Listen and repeat," is divided into four different parts:

1. The sound only
2. The sound in syllables
3. The sound in words
4. Write down the words you hear

AUDIO 32.2

1. Écoutez **le son ouille** et répétez après moi.
   *Listen to the sound **ouille** and repeat after me.*

→ *A good way to explain this sound is to pronounce **ou** + the beginning of "**yes**" in English. I like to explain as **ou + a rolling y**.*

ouil – ouille

AUDIO 32.3

2. Écoutez **le son ouille** dans **les différentes syllabes** et répétez après moi.
   *Listen to the sound **ouille** in the different syllables and repeat after me.*

bouille – douille – fouille – jouille – louille – mouille – nouille – pouille –
rouille – souille – touille – vouille – zouille

3. Écoutez **les différents mots** incluant le son **ouille** et répétez après moi.
*Listen to the different words including the sound **ouille** and repeat after me.*

Une bouilloire
Du brouillard
Un brouillon
Douillet
Fouiller

Une gargouille
Gargouiller
Gribouiller
Une patrouille
Se débrouiller

4. Écrivez **les mots** que vous entendez. Si vous ne comprenez pas le mot complet, écrivez une ou deux syllabes.
Write down the words you hear. If you don't understand the full word, write one or two syllables.

1.

2. Du

3. Une

4. Le

5.

6. Une

7. Des

8. Une

9.

10. La

VOCABULARY

Bouillir v | *To boil*
Une bouilloire nf | *A kettle*
Du bouillon nm | *Broth*
Du brouillard nm | *Fog*
Un brouillon nm | *A draft*
Une citrouille nf | *A pumpkin*
Douillet – Douillette adj | *Cozy*
Le fenouil nm | *Fennel*
Fouiller v | *To rummage*
Une gargouille nf | *A gargoyle*

Gargouiller v | *To gurgle*
Gazouiller v | *To babble*
Une grenouille nf | *A frog*
Gribouiller v | *To scribble*
Des nouilles nf | *Noodles*
Une patrouille nf | *A patrol*
Une ratatouille nf | *A ratatouille*
Rouiller v | *To rust*
Se débrouiller v | *To get by*
La trouille nf | *Fear*

UNE VISITE AU MUSÉE

A VISIT TO THE MUSEUM

33

AUDIO 33.1 ◄))

1. **Écoutez l'audio** et **lisez l'histoire** en même temps.
   Listen to the audio and read the story at the same time.

Une visite au musée

La classe de ma fille va visiter un musée aujourd'hui. Son professeur m'a demandé de les accompagner et j'ai accepté. Je ne travaille jamais le lundi donc je suis libre toute la journée. On doit être à l'école vers 7 heures et demie pour organiser la journée. Deux autres parents seront avec nous, donc on sera 4 adultes au total. Chaque adulte sera responsable d'un groupe de 5 enfants. Le budget de l'école est limité donc on va prendre les transports en commun. Le musée qu'ils ont choisi cette année est le musée des trains. On va voir de vieilles locomotives et comment elles fonctionnaient à l'époque. Ça sera très intéressant pour les enfants vu qu'il y a beaucoup de trains qui passent dans la ville. Le musée vient d'ajouter des activités interactives donc les enfants seront bien occupés pendant toute la visite.

TRANSLATION

A Visit to the Museum

My daughter's class is going to visit a museum today. Her teacher asked me to accompany them, and I accepted. I never work on Mondays, so I'm free all day. We have to be at school around 7:30 a.m. to organize the day. Two other parents will be with us so that we will be 4 adults in total. Each adult will be responsible for a group of 5 children. The school budget is limited, so we will use public transport. The museum they chose this year is the train museum. We will see old locomotives and how they worked back then. It will be very interesting for children as there are many trains passing through the city. The museum has just added interactive activities, so the children will be kept busy throughout the visit.

2. **Écoutez l'audio 33.1** et **numérotez les phrases de 1 à 11 pour les remettre dans l'ordre.**
   Listen to the audio 33.1 and number the sentences from 1 to 11 to put them in order.

   – Je ne travaille jamais le lundi donc je suis libre toute la journée.

   – On va voir de vieilles locomotives et comment elles fonctionnaient à l'époque.

- Son professeur m'a demandé de les accompagner et j'ai accepté.

- Deux autres parents seront avec nous, donc on sera 4 adultes au total.

- Le musée vient d'ajouter des activités interactives donc les enfants seront bien occupés pendant toute la visite.

- Chaque adulte sera responsable d'un groupe de 5 enfants.

- Ça sera très intéressant pour les enfants vu qu'il y a beaucoup de trains qui passent dans la ville.

- La classe de ma fille va visiter un musée aujourd'hui.

- On doit être à l'école vers 7 heures et demie pour organiser la journée.

- Le budget de l'école est limité donc on va prendre les transports en commun.

- Le musée qu'ils ont choisi cette année est le musée des trains.

AUDIO 33.2 ◀ﬂ))

VOCABULARY

Une visite nf | *A visit*
Un musée nm | *A museum*
Une classe nf | *A class*
Une fille nf | *A daughter*
Visiter v | *To visit*
Un professeur nm | *A professor*
Accompagner v | *To accompany*
Accepter v | *To accept*
Travailler v | *To work*
Le lundi nm | *Monday*
Libre adj | *Free*
Une journée nf | *A day*
À l'école | *At school*
Organiser v | *To organize*
Un parent nm | *A parent*
Un – Une adulte n | *An adult*
Au total adv | *In total*

Responsable adj | *Responsible*
Un groupe nm | *A group*
Un enfant nm | *A child*
Un budget nm | *A budget*
Être limité – limitée v | *To be limited*
Les transports en commun nm |
Public transport
Un train nm | *A train*
Une vieille locomotive adj + nf |
An old locomotive
Fonctionner v | *To work*
À l'époque | *Back then*
Intéressant – Intéressante adj | *Interesting*
Une ville nf | *A city*
Une activité interactive nf + adj |
An interactive activity
Occupé – Occupée adj | *Busy*

UNE PROMENADE EN FORÊT
A WALK IN THE FOREST

34

What is a Liaison?

A liaison in French is when the final silent consonant of a word is pronounced because the following word begins with a vowel or a silent "h." This helps make the pronunciation of groups of words more fluid.

Here are the three different types of liaisons we will focus on in this exercise:

AUDIO 34.1 ◄))

The Z Sound

The **Z sound** happens when the final consonant is an **s** and the next word begins with a vowel or a silent h.

Les yeux = Les Zyeux
Eyes

The T Sound

The **T sound** happens when the final consonant is a **t** and the next word begins with a vowel or a silent h.

C'est une belle journée. = C'est Tune belle journée.
It's a beautiful day.

The N Sound

The **N sound** happens when the final consonant is a **n** and the next word begins with a vowel or a silent h.

Un œil = Un Nœil
An eye

AUDIO 34.2 ◄))

1. **Écoutez l'audio** et soulignez **les liaisons** comme dans les exemples ci-dessus.
   Listen to the audio and underline the liaisons like in the examples above.

Une promenade en forêt

Louis et son adorable petit chien sont en train de se promener dans la forêt. La forêt est à quelques minutes de sa maison. Il n'a même pas besoin de conduire pour leurs promenades quotidiennes. Cette forêt est incroyable. Les arbres sont immenses et il y a plein d'oiseaux qui chantent. Après quelques minutes de marche, Louis aperçoit quelque chose qui bouge au loin. C'est un petit groupe de cerfs. Les animaux le regardent pendant un instant avant de disparaître dans les bois. Encore heureux que son chien ne les a pas vus ! C'est une journée parfaite pour une longue balade.

TRANSLATION

A Walk in the Forest

Louis and his adorable little dog are walking in the forest. The forest is a few minutes from his house. He doesn't even have to drive for their daily walks. This forest is incredible. The trees are huge and there are lots of birds singing. After a few minutes of walking, Louis sees something moving in the distance. It's a small group of deer. The animals stare at him for a moment before disappearing into the woods. Good thing that his dog didn't see them! It's a perfect day for a long walk.

AUDIO 34.3 ◀))

VOCABULARY

Un œil – Des yeux nm | *Eye(s)*
Une belle journée adj + nf | *A beautiful day*
Une promenade nf | *A walk*
Adorable adj | *Adorable*
Petit – Petite adj | *Little*
Un chien nm | *A dog*
Se promener v | *To walk*
La forêt nf | *The forest*
Une maison nf | *A house*
Conduire v | *To drive*
Une promenade nf | *A walk*
Quotidien – Quotidienne adj | *Daily*
Incroyable adj | *Incredible*
Un arbre nm | *A tree*
Immense adj | *Huge*
Un oiseau nm | *A bird*

Chanter v | *To sing*
Une marche nf | *A walk*
Apercevoir v | *To see*
Bouger v | *To move*
Au loin adv | *In the distance*
Un petit groupe adj + nm | *A little group*
Un cerf nm | *A deer*
Un animal – Des animaux nm |
An animal – Animals
Regarder v | *To stare*
Un instant nm | *A moment*
Disparaître v | *To disappear*
Les bois nm | *The woods*
Une journée nf | *A day*
Parfait – Parfaite adj | *Perfect*
Une longue balade adj + nm | *A long walk*

QUEL MOT EST-CE QUE JE PRONONCE ?
WHAT WORD DO I PRONOUNCE?

AUDIO 35.1 🔊

Écoutez **l'audio** et **entourez** le mot que je prononce. Chaque mot est répété deux fois.
La liste des mots est traduite après cet exercice.
*Listen to the audio and circle the word I say. Each word is repeated twice. The list of words is
translated after this exercise.*

1. Garde – Gourde
2. Dessus – Dessous
3. Court – Pour
4. Actif – Active
5. Adopter – Adapter
6. Savoir – Saveur
7. Amener – Emmener

8. Accent – Accès
9. Achat – Chat
10. Rue – Roue
11. Chiant – Chien
12. Long – Lent
13. Ton – Temps
14. Son – Sans

15. Peur – Pour
16. Pull – Poule
17. Mousse – Mouche
18. Sel – Seul
19. Plat – Plan
20. Poivre – Pauvre

AUDIO 35.2 🔊

VOCABULARY

Un – Une garde n | *A guard*
Une gourde nf | *A gourd*
Dessus adv | *Above*
Dessous adv | *Below*
Court – Courte adj | *Short*
Pour prep | *For*
Actif – Active adj | *Active*
Adopter v | *To adopt*
Adapter v | *To adapt*
Savoir v | *To know*
Une saveur nf | *A flavour*
Amener v | *To bring*
Emmener v | *To take away*
Un accent nm | *An accent*
Un accès nm | *An access*
Un achat nm | *A purchase*
Un chat nm | *A cat*
Une rue nf | *A street*
Une roue nf | *A wheel*
Chiant – Chiante adj | *Annoying*

Un chien nm | *A dog*
Long – Longue adj | *Long*
Lent – Lente adj | *Slow*
Ton adj | *Your*
Le temps nm | *The time*
Son adj | *His – Her*
Sans prep | *Without*
La peur nf | *Fear*
Pour prep | *For*
Un pull nm | *A sweater*
Une poule nf | *A chicken*
La mousse nf | *The foam*
Une mouche nf | *A fly*
Le sel nm | *Salt*
Seul – Seule adj | *Alone*
Un plat nm | *A dish*
Un plan nm | *A plan*
Du poivre nm | *Pepper*
Pauvre adj | *Poor*

LA LETTRE MUETTE X
THE SILENT LETTER X

36

What is a Silent Letter?

A silent letter in French is a letter that is not pronounced. A silent letter is usually at the end of a word.

The silent **x** in French is commonly found at the end of plural nouns and adjectives as well as at specific words, so let's see them!

Here are the four types of words where you can find the silent letter **x** in French:

AUDIO 36.1 ◄))

At the end of singular nouns

La paix nf | *Peace*
Un prix nm | *A price*
Un choix nm | *A choice*

AUDIO 36.2 ◄))

At the end of plural nouns

Des bijoux nm | *Jewels*
Des genoux nm | *Knees*
Des hiboux nm | *Owls*

AUDIO 36.3 ◄))

At the end of adjectives

Jaloux adj | *Jealous*
Délicieux adj | *Delicious*

AUDIO 36.4 ◄))

When a verb is conjugated with je – tu

Je peux v | *I can*
Tu veux v | *You want*

AUDIO 36.5 ◄))

1. Écoutez ces 20 phrases et **entourez les mots** où **la lettre x est muette**.
   *Listen to these 20 sentences and circle the words where the letter **x** is silent.*

1. Le prix de ce lit est beaucoup trop cher.

2. Ce que tu dis est faux.

3. La croix est tombée pendant la nuit.

4. Les bijoux de ma mère ont disparu.

5. Les Jeux Olympiques se sont déroulés à Paris.

6. Tous les feux de la ville sont en panne.

7. Mon chien devient vieux.

8. J'ai les cheveux longs depuis toujours.

9. Il est tellement heureux depuis qu'il a changé de travail.

10. Mes deux frères sont célibataires.

11. C'est généreux de ta part.

12. Il est nerveux de parler en public.

13. Les eaux usées ne sont pas bien traitées.

14. Tu es sérieux ?

15. Je n'ai pas le choix.

16. Mon époux sera présent à la réunion.

17. Je mange des noix tous les jours.

18. Ce coussin est vraiment doux.

19. Qu'est-ce que tu veux faire aujourd'hui ?

20. Mon mari a les cheveux roux.

TRANSLATION

1. *The price of this bed is way too expensive.*

2. *What you say is false.*

3. *The cross fell during the night.*

4. *My mother's jewelry is missing.*

5. *The Olympic Games took place in Paris.*

6. *All the city's lights are out of order.*

7. *My dog is getting old.*

8. *I've always had long hair.*

9. *He is so happy since he changed jobs.*

10. *My two brothers are single.*

11. *That's generous of you.*

12. *He is nervous about speaking in public.*

13. *Wastewater is not treated well.*

14. *Are you serious?*

15. *I have no choice.*

16. *My spouse will be present at the meeting.*

17. *I eat nuts every day.*

18. *This cushion is really soft.*

19. *What do you want to do today?*

20. *My husband has red hair.*

VOCABULARY

La paix nf | *Peace*

Un prix nm | *A price*

Un choix nm | *A choice*

Des bijoux nm | *Jewels*

Des genoux nm | *Knees*

Des hiboux nm | *Owls*

Jaloux adj | *Jealous*

Délicieux adj | *Delicious*

Je peux (Pouvoir) v | *I can (To be able to)*

Tu veux (Vouloir) v | *You want (To want)*

Un lit nm | *A bed*

Cher – Chère adj | *Expensive*

Dire v | *To say*

Faux – Fausse adj | *False*

Une croix nf | *A cross*

La nuit nf | *The night*

Une mère nf | *A mother*

Disparaître v | *To disappear*

Les Jeux Olympiques nm | *The Olympic Games*

Se dérouler v | *To take place*

Un feu nm | *A city light*

Une ville nf | *A city*

Être en panne v | *To be out of order*

Un chien nm | *A dog*

Devenir v | *To become*

Vieux – Vieille adj | *Old*

Les cheveux nm | *Hair*

Long – Longue adj | *Long*

Heureux – Heureuse adj | *Happy*

Le travail nm | *Work*

Deux n | *Two*

Un frère nm | *A brother*

Célibataire adj | *Single*

Généreux – Généreuse adj | *Generous*

Nerveux – Nerveuse adj | *Nervous*

Parler v | *To speak*

Les eaux usées nf | *Wastewater*

Traiter v | *To treat*

Sérieux – Sérieuse adj | *Serious*

Un choix nm | *A choice*

Un époux nm | *A spouse*

Une réunion nf | *A meeting*

Manger v | *To eat*

Une noix nf | *A nut*

Un coussin nm | *A cushion*

Doux – Douce adj | *Soft*

Un mari nm | *A husband*

Roux – Rousse adj | *Red (for hair)*

L'INCIDENT AU SUPERMARCHÉ
THE INCIDENT AT THE SUPERMARKET

37

AUDIO 37.1 ◄))

1. **Écoutez l'audio** et **lisez l'histoire** en même temps.
   Listen to the audio and read the story at the same time.

L'incident au supermarché

Il y a quelques jours, j'étais au supermarché et j'ai renversé une pile de boîtes de conserve. Je n'arrive toujours pas à y croire. J'ai vraiment honte. Je marchais devant les frigos quand une personne avec un caddie est arrivée de l'autre côté. J'ai fait quelques pas en arrière pour lui laisser assez de place pour passer. Je n'ai pas fait attention à ce qu'il y avait derrière moi. Quand j'ai senti quelque chose contre mon dos, c'était déjà trop tard. J'ai reculé dans une grande pile de boîtes de conserve parfaitement empilées. Elles sont tombées et ont roulé dans toutes les directions. Tout le monde me regardait. J'étais tellement gênée ! Un employé du magasin est arrivé en moins d'une minute. Il m'a rassuré que cela arrivait souvent. Il a commencé à ramasser les boîtes de conserve mais certaines étaient trop abîmées. Je voulais les acheter mais il a dit que ce n'était pas nécessaire. Je suis gênée rien que d'y repenser.

TRANSLATION

The Incident at the Supermarket

A few days ago, I was at the supermarket, and I knocked over a pile of cans. I still can't believe it. I'm really ashamed. I was walking past the fridges when a person with a shopping cart came up from the other side. I took a few steps back to give him enough room to pass. I didn't pay attention to what was behind me. When I felt something against my back, it was already too late. I backed into a large pile of perfectly stacked cans. They fell and rolled in all directions. Everyone was looking at me. I was so embarrassed! A store employee arrived in less than a minute. He reassured me that this happened often. He started to collect the cans, but some were too damaged. I wanted to buy them, but he said it wasn't necessary. I'm embarrassed to think about it.

2. **Écoutez l'audio 37.1** et ajoutez **les mots manquants**.
Listen to the audio 37.1 and add the missing words.

L'incident au supermarché

Il y a quelques _____, j'étais au supermarché et j'ai renversé une _____ de boîtes de conserve. Je n'arrive toujours pas à y _____.
J'ai vraiment honte. Je marchais devant les _____ quand une personne avec un caddie est arrivée de l'autre côté. J'ai fait quelques _____ en arrière pour lui laisser assez de _____ pour passer. Je n'ai pas fait attention à ce qu'il y avait derrière _____. Quand j'ai senti quelque chose contre mon _____, c'était déjà trop tard. J'ai reculé dans une _____ pile de boîtes de conserve parfaitement empilées. Elles sont tombées et ont roulé dans toutes les _____. Tout le monde me regardait. J'étais tellement gênée ! Un _____ du magasin est arrivé en moins d'une minute. Il m'a rassuré que cela arrivait _____. Il a commencé à ramasser les boîtes de conserve mais certaines étaient trop abîmées. Je voulais les _____ mais il a dit que ce n'était pas nécessaire. Je suis gênée rien que d'y _____.

AUDIO 37.2 ◀))

VOCABULARY

Un incident nm | *An incident*
Un supermarché nm | *A supermarket*
Renverser v | *To knock over*
Une pile nf | *A pile*
Une boîte de conserve nf | *A can*
Croire v | *To believe*
Avoir honte v | *To be ashamed*
Marcher v | *To walk*
Un frigo nm | *A fridge*
Une personne nf | *A person*
Un caddie nm | *A shopping cart*
Un pas nm | *A step*
En arrière adv | *Back*
Laisser v | *To give*
Une place nf | *Room*
Passer v | *To pass*

Faire attention v | *To pay attention*
Derrière adv | *Behind*
Sentir v | *To feel*
Le dos nm | *The back*
Reculer v | *To back*
Empilé – Empilée adj | *Stacked*
Être tombé – tombée v | *To fall*
Rouler v | *To roll*
Une direction nf | *A direction*
Être gêné – gênée v | *To be embarassed*
Un employé nm | *An employee*
Rassurer v | *To reassure*
Ramasser v | *To collect*
Être abîmé – abîmée v | *To be damaged*
Nécessaire adv | *Necessary*

LES SONS EUILLE – EILLE – AILLE – ILLE – OUILLE

38

THE SOUNDS EUILLE – EILLE – AILLE – ILLE – OUILLE

In Chapter 14, you have learned to recognize **the sound euille**, **the sound eille** in Chapter 18, **the sound aille** in Chapter 22, **the sound ille** in Chapter 28, and **the sound ouille** in Chapter 32. It's time to review them together in an exercise!

Here are the different spellings for each sound:

The Sound euille

euille – euil – ueil – ueille – œil

The Sound eille

eil – eille

The Sound aille

ail – aille

The Sound ille

ille

The Sound ouille

ouil – ouille

AUDIO 38.1 ◄))

Écoutez les différentes phrases et ajoutez **le bon son** à chaque partie manquante.
Listen to the different sentences and add the correct sound to each missing part.

1. Les f   s commencent à changer de couleur.

2. La gren   saute dans l'étang.

3. Je trav   sur mon projet avec ma collègue.

4. Le pap   on s'est posé sur la chaise de jardin.

5. Ma f   adore la glace à la van   .

6. Le fermier donne de la p   aux chevaux.

7. J'ai quelque chose dans l'   .

8. Toute ma fam   se réunit pour fêter Noël.

9. Est-ce que tu as vu ma bout   d'eau ?

10. On a un plat de n   s pour le déjeuner.

11. Le jardinier t   les arbres du parc.

12. L'ab   va de fleur en fleur.

13. Je vais c   lir des fraises dans le jardin.

14. On se rév   vers 7 heures tous les matins.

15. Mon or   me fait un peu mal aujourd'hui.

16. Le gagnant a reçu une méd   d'or.

17. Il s'hab   rapidement pour aller à l'école.

18. J'adore la ratat   !

19. Le sol   br   dans le ciel.

20. Ajoute un peu d'   pour plus de saveur.

TRANSLATION

1. *The leaves begin to change color.*
2. *The frog jumps into the pond.*
3. *I am working on my project with my colleague.*
4. *The butterfly landed on the garden chair.*
5. *My daughter loves vanilla ice cream.*
6. *The farmer gives straw to the horses.*
7. *I have something in my eye.*
8. *My whole family comes together to celebrate Christmas.*
9. *Have you seen my water bottle?*
10. *We have a noodle dish for lunch.*
11. *The gardener prunes the trees in the park.*
12. *The bee goes from flower to flower.*
13. *I'm going to pick strawberries in the garden.*
14. *We wake up around 7 a.m. every morning.*
15. *My ear hurts a little today.*
16. *The winner received a gold medal.*

17.   *He gets dressed quickly to go to school.*

18.   *I love ratatouille!*

19.   *The sun is shining in the sky.*

20.   *Add a little garlic for more flavor.*

VOCABULARY

Une feuille nf | *A leaf*
Commencer v | *To begin*
Changer v | *To change*
Une couleur nf | *A color*
Une grenouille nf | *A frog*
Sauter v | *To jump*
Un étang nm | *A pond*
Travailler v | *To work*
Un projet nm | *A project*
Une collègue nf | *A colleague*
Un papillon nm | *A butterfly*
Se poser v | *To land*
Une chaise de jardin nf | *A garden chair*
Une fille nf | *A daughter*
Adorer v | *To love*
De la glace nf | *Ice cream*
La vanille nf | *Vanilla*
Un fermier nm | *A farmer*
Donner v | *To give*
De la paille nf | *Straw*
Un cheval – Des chevaux nm |
A horse – Horses
Quelque chose pr | *Something*
Un œil nm | *An eye*
Une famille nf | *A family*
Se réunir v | *To come together*
Fêter v | *To celebrate*
Noël nm | *Christmas*
Une bouteille d'eau nf | *A water bottle*

Un plat nm | *A dish*
Des nouilles nf | *Noodles*
Un déjeuner nm | *A lunch*
Un jardinier nm | *A gardener*
Tailler v | *To prune*
Un arbre nm | *A tree*
Un parc nm | *A park*
Une abeille nf | *A bee*
Une fleur nf | *A flower*
Cueillir v | *To pick*
Une fraise nf | *A strawberry*
Un jardin nm | *A garden*
Se réveiller v | *To wake up*
Une oreille nf | *An ear*
Faire mal v | *To hurt*
Un gagnant nm | *A winner*
Recevoir v | *To receive*
Une médaille d'or nf | *A gold medal*
S'habiller v | *To get dressed*
Une école nf | *A school*
Adorer v | *To love*
Une ratatouille nf | *Ratatouille*
Le soleil nm | *The sun*
Briller v | *To shine*
Le ciel nm | *The sky*
Ajouter v | *To add*
De l'ail nm | *Garlic*
Une saveur nf | *A flavor*

LE MARATHON
THE MARATHON

39

AUDIO 39.1 ◄))

1. **Écoutez l'audio** et **lisez l'histoire** en même temps.
   Listen to the audio and read the story at the same time.

Le marathon

Mon frère est très athlétique. Il court presque tous les jours. Son prochain objectif est de courir un marathon. Un marathon fait 42 kilomètres donc c'est définitivement un exploit sportif. Il a gagné plusieurs courses de 10 et 20 kilomètres mais il n'a jamais couru aussi longtemps. Il s'entraîne beaucoup pour être prêt. Chaque semaine, il court de plus en plus longtemps pour améliorer son endurance. En plus de ça, il fait aussi attention à son alimentation. Il mange beaucoup de légumes et de protéines. Il est vraiment motivé ! Toute la famille le soutient et on sera tous là le jour de la course pour l'encourager. Le grand jour est dans deux mois. On a tous hâte de le voir franchir la ligne d'arrivée.

TRANSLATION

The Marathon

My brother is very athletic. He runs almost every day. His next goal is to run a marathon. A marathon is 42 kilometres, so it's definitely a sporting achievement. He won several 10 and 20 kilometre races but never ran that long. He practices a lot to be ready. Every week, he runs longer and longer to improve his endurance. In addition to that, he also pays attention to his diet. He eats a lot of vegetables and proteins. He is really motivated! The whole family supports him, and we will all be there on race day to cheer him on. The big day is in two months. We all can't wait to see him cross the finish line.

2. **Écoutez l'audio 39.1** et **numérotez les phrases de 1 à 13 pour les remettre dans l'ordre.**
   Listen to the audio 39.1 and number the sentences from 1 to 13 to put them in order.

Le marathon

– Il a gagné plusieurs courses de 10 et 20 kilomètres mais il n'a jamais couru aussi longtemps.

– Mon frère est très athlétique.

– Un marathon fait 42 kilomètres donc c'est définitivement un exploit sportif.

– Il est vraiment motivé !

– Il court presque tous les jours.

– Il s'entraîne beaucoup pour être prêt.

– Il mange beaucoup de légumes et de protéines.

– On a tous hâte de le voir franchir la ligne d'arrivée.

– Chaque semaine, il court de plus en plus longtemps pour améliorer son endurance.

– Toute la famille le soutient et on sera tous là le jour de la course pour l'encourager.

– En plus de ça, il fait aussi attention à son alimentation.

– Le grand jour est dans deux mois.

– Son prochain objectif est de courir un marathon.

AUDIO 39.2 ◄))

VOCABULARY

Un marathon nm | *A marathon*
Un frère nm | *A brother*
Athlétique adj | *Athletic*
Courir v | *To run*
Un objectif nm | *A goal*
Un kilomètre nm | *A kilometre*
Un exploit sportif nm | *A sporting achievement*
Gagner v | *To win*
Une course nf | *A race*
S'entraîner v | *To practice*
Prêt – Prête adj | *Ready*
Améliorer v | *To improve*
De l'endurance nf | *Endurance*

Une alimentation nf | *A diet*
Manger v | *To eat*
Des légumes nm | *Vegetables*
Des protéines nf | *Proteins*
Être motivé – motivée v | *To be motivated*
Une famille nf | *A family*
Soutenir v | *To support*
Encourager v | *To cheer*
Le grand jour nm | *The big day*
Avoir hâte v | *Can't wait*
Franchir v | *To cross*
La ligne d'arrivée nf | *The finish line*

UN VOYAGE EN TRAIN
A TRAIN JOURNEY

40

What is a Liaison?

A liaison in French is when the final silent consonant of a word is pronounced because the following word begins with a vowel or a silent "h." This helps make the pronunciation of groups of words more fluid.

Here are the three different types of liaisons we will focus on in this exercise:

AUDIO 40.1 ◄))

The Z Sound

The **Z sound** happens when the final consonant is an **s** and the next word begins with a vowel or a silent h.

Mes enfants = Mes Zenfants
My children

The T Sound

The **T sound** happens when the final consonant is a **t** and the next word begins with a vowel or a silent h.

Cet outil = Cet Toutil
This tool

The N Sound

The **N sound** happens when the final consonant is a **n** and the next word begins with a vowel or a silent h.

Mon armoire = Mon Narmoire
My wardrobe

AUDIO 40.2 ◄))

1. **Écoutez l'audio** et soulignez **les liaisons** comme dans les exemples ci-dessus.
   Listen to the audio and underline the liaisons like in the examples above.

Un voyage en train

Cet après-midi, mon amie et moi avons pris le train pour aller à la mer. On est arrivées vers treize heures. Le voyage en train n'a pris qu'une heure et n'a coûté que trois euros. Cela en vaut vraiment la peine. On compte trouver un hôtel pour rester jusque demain. Il fait trop froid pour nager mais on aime beaucoup marcher. La plage est interminable donc on peut marcher pendant des heures. Vers dix-sept heures, on va certainement aller prendre un café et chercher un restaurant pour le dîner. On a envie de manger italien, probablement des pâtes ou des pizzas.

TRANSLATION

A Train Journey

This afternoon, my friend and I took the train to the sea. We arrived around one p.m. The train journey took only an hour and cost three euros. It's definitely worth it. We plan to find a hotel to stay until tomorrow. It's too cold to swim, but we really like walking. The beach is endless, so you can walk for hours. Around 5 p.m., we'll definitely get a coffee and look for a restaurant for dinner. We want to eat Italian, probably pasta or pizza.

AUDIO 40.3 ◀))

VOCABULARY

Un – Une enfant n | *A child*
Un outil nm | *A tool*
Une armoire nf | *A wardrobe*
Un voyage nm | *A journey*
Un après-midi nm | *An afternoon*
Un – Une amie n | *A friend*
Un train nm | *A train*
La mer nf | *The sea*
Prendre v | *To take*
Coûter v | *To cost*
Un euro nm | *A euro*
En valoir la peine v | *To be worth it*
Compter v | *To plan*
Trouver v | *To find*
Un hôtel nm | *A hotel*

Rester v | *To stay*
Faire froid v | *To be cold*
Nager v | *To swim*
Marcher v | *To walk*
Une plage nf | *A beach*
Interminable adj | *Endless*
Décider v | *To decide*
Prendre un café v | *To have a coffee*
Chercher v | *To look for*
Un restaurant nm | *A restaurant*
Le dîner nm | *Dinner*
Italien adj | *Italian*
Des pâtes nf | *Pasta*
Des pizzas nf | *Pizzas*

LES URGENCES
THE ER

41

AUDIO 41.1 ◀))

1. **Écoutez l'audio** et **lisez l'histoire** en même temps.
   Listen to the audio and read the story at the same time.

Les urgences

Je suis aux urgences car je me suis foulé la cheville. C'était un accident vraiment bête. Pour accéder à mon jardin, je dois descendre quelques marches. Ce matin, alors que je portais un panier de linge, mon pied a glissé sur la dernière marche. J'ai tout de suite senti une douleur intense à la cheville. Après quelques minutes, j'ai pu me lever et appeler mon voisin. Il m'a aidé à marcher jusqu'à sa voiture. Les urgences de l'hôpital sont seulement à 5 minutes de chez moi. Je suis aux urgences depuis un peu plus d'une heure. J'ai attendu mon tour patiemment. Il n'y avait pas beaucoup de monde donc j'ai vu un docteur assez vite. L'infirmière m'a envoyé faire une radiographie pour vérifier que je n'avais pas de fracture. Heureusement, c'est seulement une entorse. Je vais porter une attelle pendant une semaine et utiliser des béquilles pour marcher. Plus de peur que de mal.

TRANSLATION

The ER

I'm in the emergency room because I sprained my ankle. It was a really stupid accident. To access my garden, I have to go down a few steps. This morning, while carrying a basket of laundry, my foot slipped on the last step. I immediately felt intense pain in my ankle. After a few minutes, I got up and called my neighbor. He helped me walk to his car. The hospital emergency room is only 5 minutes from my house. I've been in the emergency room for a little over an hour. I waited my turn patiently. There weren't many people there, so I saw a doctor pretty quickly. The nurse sent me for an x-ray to check that I didn't have a fracture. Fortunately, it's only a sprain. I will wear a splint for a week and use crutches to walk. More fear than harm.

2. **Écoutez l'audio 41.1** et ajoutez **les mots manquants**.
Listen to the audio 41.1 and add the missing words.

Les urgences

Je suis aux urgences car je me suis foulé la _____ . C'était un accident

vraiment _____ . Pour accéder à mon _____ , je dois descendre

quelques _____ . Ce matin, alors que je portais un panier de linge, mon

_____ a glissé sur la dernière marche. J'ai tout de suite senti une douleur intense

à la cheville. Après quelques _____ , j'ai pu me lever et appeler mon voisin. Il m'a

aidé à marcher jusqu'à sa _____ . Les urgences de l'hôpital sont seulement à

5 _____ de chez moi. Je suis aux urgences depuis un peu plus d'une heure.

J'ai attendu mon tour patiemment. Il n'y avait pas beaucoup de _____ donc

j'ai vu un docteur assez vite. L'infirmière m'a envoyé _____ une radiographie

pour vérifier que je n'avais pas de fracture. Heureusement, c'est seulement une entorse. Je

vais _____ une attelle pendant une semaine et utiliser des béquilles pour

_____ . Plus de peur que de mal.

AUDIO 41.2 ◀))

VOCABULARY

Les urgences nf | *The ER/The emergency room*
Se fouler v | *To sprain*
Une cheville nf | *An ankle*
Un accident nm | *An accident*
Bête adj | *Stupid*
Accéder v | *To access*
Un jardin nm | *A garden*
Descendre v | *To go down*
Une marche nf | *A step*
Porter v | *To carry*
Un panier de linge nm | *A basket of laundry*
Un pied nm | *A foot*
Glisser v | *To slip*
Sentir v | *To feel*
Une douleur intense nf + adj | *An intense pain*
Se lever v | *To get up*
Appeler v | *To call*

Un voisin nm | *A neighbor*
Marcher v | *To walk*
Une voiture nf | *A car*
Un hôpital nm | *A hospital*
Attendre v | *To wait*
Un tour nm | *A turn*
Un docteur nm | *A doctor*
Une infirmière nf | *A nurse*
Une radiographie nf | *An x-ray*
Vérifier v | *To check*
Une fracture nf | *A fracture*
Une entorse nf | *A sprain*
Porter v | *To wear*
Une attelle nf | *A splint*
Utiliser v | *To use*
Des béquilles nf | *Crutches*

LE SON R
THE SOUND R

42

R has always a special place among French learners since it's such a hard sound to pronounce. In this exercise, we are going to work on the sound alone with vowels, then by syllables, before moving to complete words.

AUDIO 42.1 ◀»

1. Écoutez **le son r** avec différentes voyelles et répétez après moi.
   Listen to the sound r with different vowels and repeat after me.

   ra – re – ri – ro – ru

AUDIO 42.2 ◀»

2. Écoutez **le son r** dans **les différentes syllabes** et répétez après moi.
   Listen to the sound r in the different syllables and repeat after me.

R + A

   bra – cra – dra – fra – gra – pra – tra – vra – zra

R + E

   bre – cre – dre – fre – gre – pre – tre – vre – zre

R + I

   bri – cri – dri – fri – gri – pri – tri – vri – zri

R + O

   bro – cro – dro – fro – gro – pro – tro – vro – zro

R + U

   bru – cru – dru – fru – gru – pru – tru – vru – zru

3. Écoutez **les différents mots** incluant **r** et répétez après moi.
   *Listen to the different words including **r** and repeat after me.*

Un anniversaire	Une gare
Artificiel	Hier
Avril	La maire
Une barre	La mémoire
Un bras	Un mur
Un bureau	Une narine
De la crème	Un ours
Dur	Ouvrir
Faire	Parler
La France	Prêt

4. Écrivez **les mots** que vous entendez. Si vous ne comprenez pas le mot complet,
   écrivez une ou deux syllabes.
   Write down the words you hear. If you don't understand the full word, write one or
   two syllables.

1. Un	11.
2. Un	12. Une
3. Une	13. Un
4. Un	14.
5. Une	15. Un
6. Le	16. Un
7. Un	17. Un
8. Une	18. Un
9.	19.
10. Un	20. Un

VOCABULARY

Un anniversaire nm | *A birthday*
Un arbre nm | *A tree*
Un arc nm | *An arc*
Artificiel – Artificielle adj | *Artificial*
Avril nm | *April*
Une carotte nf | *A carrot*
Un carré nm | *A square*
Une barre nf | *A bar*
Un bras nm | *An arm*
Un bureau nm | *A desk*
De la crème nf | *Cream*
Dur – Dure adj | *Hard*
Une erreur nf | *A mistake*
Faire v | *To do*
Le fer nm | *Iron*
La France nf | *France*
Une gare nf | *A train station*
Hier adv | *Yesterday*
Un jardin nm | *A garden*
Une larme nf | *A tear*

Lourd – Lourde adj | *Heavy*
La maire nf | *The mayor*
La mémoire nf | *The memory*
Un miroir nm | *A mirror*
Un mur nm | *A wall*
Une narine nf | *A nostril*
Un ours nm | *A bear*
Ouvrir v | *To open*
Parler v | *To speak*
Partager v | *To share*
Une porte nf | *A door*
Prêt – Prête adj | *Ready*
Un rideau nm | *A curtain*
Rire v | *To laugh*
Un robinet nm | *A faucet*
Un rond nm | *A round*
Un sourire nm | *A smile*
Un travail nm | *A job*
Trois nm | *Three*
Un verre nm | *A glass*

NOTRE JOURNÉE À PARIS
OUR DAY IN PARIS

43

1. **Écoutez l'audio** et **lisez l'histoire** en même temps.
   Listen to the audio and read the story at the same time.

Notre journée à Paris

C'est la première fois qu'on visite Paris. On mange notre petit déjeuner avant d'attaquer la journée. On a un million de choses à voir. On va commencer par la tour Eiffel. On a acheté des tickets en ligne pour aller tout en haut. On a hâte ! Une fois la visite de la tour Eiffel terminée, on se dirigera vers l'Arc de Triomphe. Pour le déjeuner, on cherchera un restaurant près de l'Arc de Triomphe. Ça ne devrait pas être difficile à trouver. Une fois le déjeuner fini, on ira visiter le musée du Louvre. Je veux voir la Joconde et les œuvres grecques. Je pense qu'on sera fatigués après le Louvre donc on ira sûrement boire un café avant de faire un tour en bateau mouche sur la Seine. Ce soir, on a deux billets pour le Moulin Rouge. On a une longue journée devant nous !

TRANSLATION

Our Day in Paris

This is our first time visiting Paris. We eat our breakfast before starting the day. We have a million things to see. We will start with the Eiffel Tower. We bought tickets online to go to the top. We can't wait! Once the visit to the Eiffel Tower is over, we will head to the Arc de Triomphe. For lunch, we will look for a restaurant near the Arc de Triomphe. It shouldn't be hard to find. Once lunch is over, we will visit the Louvre Museum. I want to see the Mona Lisa and the Greek works. I think we'll be tired after the Louvre, so we'll probably go have a coffee before taking a riverboat ride on the Seine. Tonight, we have two tickets to the Moulin Rouge. We have a long day ahead of us!

2. **Écoutez l'audio 43.1** et **numérotez les phrases de 1 à 14 pour les remettre dans l'ordre.**
   Listen to the audio 43.1 and number the sentences from 1 to 14 to put them in order.

Notre journée à Paris

- Une fois la visite de la tour Eiffel terminée, on se dirigera vers l'Arc de Triomphe.

- Une fois le déjeuner fini, on ira visiter le musée du Louvre.

– On a un million de choses à voir.

– On va commencer par la tour Eiffel.

– On a une longue journée devant nous !

– On a hâte !

– Ce soir, on a deux billets pour le Moulin Rouge.

– C'est la première fois qu'on visite Paris.

– Pour le déjeuner, on cherchera un restaurant près de l'Arc de Triomphe.

– Je veux voir la Joconde et les œuvres grecques.

– On a acheté des tickets en ligne pour aller tout en haut.

– Ça ne devrait pas être difficile à trouver.

– Je pense qu'on sera fatigués après le Louvre donc on ira sûrement boire un café avant de faire un tour en bateau mouche sur la Seine.

– On mange notre petit déjeuner avant d'attaquer la journée.

AUDIO 43.2 ◀))

VOCABULARY

Une journée nf | *A day*
La première fois adj + nf | *A first day*
Visiter v | *To visit*
Un petit déjeuner nm | *A breakfast*
Attaquer v | *To start*
Un million nm | *A million*
Une chose à voir | *A thing to see*
La tour Eiffel nf | *The Eiffel Tower*
Un ticket nm | *A ticket*
En ligne adv | *Online*
Avoir hâte v | *Can't wait*
Une visite nf | *A visit*
Se diriger v | *To head*

L'Arc de Triomphe nm | *The Arc of Triomphe*
Un déjeuner nm | *A lunch*
Un restaurant nm | *A restaurant*
Difficile adj | *Difficult*
Trouver v | *To find*
Le musée du Louvre nm | *The Louvre Museum*
La Joconde nf | *The Mona Lisa*
Une œuvre grecque nf + adj | *A Greek work*
Boire un café | *To drink a coffee*
Faire un tour | *To take a ride*
Un bateau mouche nm | *A riverboat*
Un billet nm | *A ticket*
Long – Longue adj | *Long*

LA LETTRE MUETTE D
THE SILENT LETTER D

44

What is a Silent Letter?

A silent letter in French is a letter that is not pronounced. A silent letter is usually at the end of a word.

The letter **d** is the least common silent letter seen in this book (after **e**, **s**, **t** and **x**).

Here are the two types of words where you can find the silent letter **d** in French:

AUDIO 44.1 ◀))

At the end of nouns and adjectives

Un pied nm | *A foot*
Un bond nm | *A jump*

Grand adj | *Tall*
Gourmand adj | *Greedy*

AUDIO 44.2 ◀))

When a verb is conjugated with il – elle – on

Il comprend v | *He understands*
Il prend v | *He takes*

Elle entend v | *She listens*
Elle se détend v | *She is relaxing*

On attend v | *We are waiting*
On reprend v | *We are restarting*

AUDIO 44.3 ◀))

1. Écoutez la différence lorsque **la lettre d** est **prononcée** et **non prononcée**.
   *Listen to the difference when the letter **d** is pronounced and not pronounced.*

Le sud – *The South*
Le nord – *The North*

AUDIO 44.4 ◀))

2. Écoutez ces 20 phrases et **entourez les mots** où **la lettre d est muette**.
   *Listen to these 20 sentences and circle the words where the letter **d** is silent.*

1. Elle s'est cassé le pied gauche.
2. Est-ce que tu as froid ?
3. Regarde ce que tu as fait.
4. Le crapaud vient de sauter dans la marre.

5. Il fait chaud aujourd'hui !

6. Il est plus grand que je ne le pensais.

7. Appelle-moi quand tu arrives.

8. On a réservé la table ronde au restaurant.

9. Les oiseaux travaillent dur pour construire leur nid.

10. Cette entreprise a été fondée il y a dix ans.

11. Qu'est-ce que tu prends pour dîner ?

12. Il y a toujours des canards dans ce parc.

13. Le nord est le contraire du sud.

14. On a trouvé un accord.

15. Elle a toujours été gourmande.

16. Il y a des travaux sur le boulevard aujourd'hui.

17. Il a un beau regard.

18. Je parle un petit peu allemand.

19. Il y a une araignée au plafond.

20. La loterie est un jeu de hasard.

TRANSLATION

1. *She broke her left foot.*

2. *Are you cold?*

3. *Look what you did.*

4. *The toad has just jumped into the pond.*

5. *It's hot today!*

6. *It's bigger than I thought.*

7. *Call me when you arrive.*

8. *We reserved the round table at the restaurant.*

9. *The birds work hard to build their nest.*

10. *This company was founded ten years ago.*

11. *What are you having for dinner?*

12. *There are always ducks in this park.*

13. *North is the opposite of south.*

14. *We reached an agreement.*

15. *She has always been greedy.*

16. *There is work on the boulevard today.*

17. *He has a beautiful look.*

18. *I speak a little German.*

19. *There's a spider on the ceiling.*

20. *The lottery is a game of chance.*

VOCABULARY

Un pied nm | *A foot*
Un bond nm | *A jump*
Grand adj | *Tall*
Gourmand adj | *Greedy*
Il comprend (Comprendre) v |
He understands (To understand)
Il prend (Prendre) v | *He takes (To take)*
Elle entend (Entendre) v |
She listens (To listen)
Elle se détend (Se détendre) v |
She is relaxing (To relax)
On attend (Attendre) v |
We are waiting (To wait)
On reprend (Reprendre) v |
We are restarting (To restart)
Le sud nm | *The South*
Le nord nm | *The North*
Se casser v | *To break*
Un pied nm | *A foot*
Gauche adj | *Left*
Froid adj | *Cold*
Regarder v | *To look*
Un crapaud nm | *A toad*
Sauter v | *To jump*
Une marre nf | *A pond*
Chaud adj | *Hot*
Penser v | *To think*
Appeler v | *To call*
Quand adv | *When*

Arriver v | *To arrive*
Réserver v | *To book*
Une table nf | *A table*
Rond adj | *Round*
Un restaurant nm | *A restaurant*
Un oiseau nm | *A bird*
Travailler v | *To work*
Dur – Dure adj | *Hard*
Construire v | *To build*
Un nid nm | *A nest*
Une entreprise nf | *A company*
Prendre v | *To take*
Un dîner nm | *A dinner*
Un canard nm | *A duck*
Un parc nm | *A park*
Le contraire nm | *The opposite*
Un accord nm | *An agreement*
Des travaux nm | *Work*
Un boulevard nm | *A boulevard*
Le regard nm | *Look*
Beau – Belle adj | *Beautiful*
Parler v | *To speak*
Allemand adj | *German*
Une araignée nf | *A spider*
Le plafond nm | *The ceiling*
La loterie nf | *The lottery*
Un jeu nm | *A game*
Le hasard nm | *Chance*

QUEL MOT EST-CE QUE JE PRONONCE ? **45**
WHAT WORD DO I PRONOUNCE?

AUDIO 45.1 ◀»)

Écoutez **l'audio** et **entourez** le mot que je prononce. Chaque mot est répété deux fois. La liste des mots est traduite après cet exercice.
Listen to the audio and circle the word I say. Each word is repeated twice. The list of words is translated after this exercise.

1. Trois – Toi
2. Langue – Longue
3. Pain – Paon
4. Je – Jeu
5. Rose – Rase
6. Dos – Doigt
7. Chaud – Chou

8. Leur – Lourd
9. Chaque – Chacun
10. Belle – Balle
11. Tout – Tôt
12. Lent – Long
13. Jeu – Joue
14. Cheveux – Chevaux

15. Paire – Par
16. Dessert – Désert
17. Quatre – Quart
18. Pâle – Paille
19. Pince – Ponce
20. Feuille – Fouille

AUDIO 45.2 ◀»)

VOCABULARY

Trois n | *Three*
Toi pr | *You*
Une langue nf | *A language*
Long – Longue adj | *Long*
Du pain nm | *Bread*
Un paon nm | *A peacock*
Je pr | *I*
Un jeu nm | *A game*
Rose adj | *Pink*
Rase (Raser) v | *To shave*
Le dos nm | *Back*
Un doigt nm | *A finger*
Chaud – Chaude adj | *Hot*
Un chou nm | *A cabbage*
Leur pr | *Their*
Lourd – Lourde adj | *Heavy*
Chaque adj | *Each*
Chacun – Chacune pr | Each
Beau – Belle adj | *Beautiful*
Une balle nf | *A ball*

Tout adj | *All*
Tôt adv | *Early*
Lent – Lente adj | *Slow*
Long – Longue adj | *Long*
Un jeu nm | *A game*
Une joue nf | *A cheek*
Des cheveux nm | *Hair*
Des chevaux nm | *Horses*
Une paire nf | *A pair*
Par prep | *By*
Un dessert nm | *A dessert*
Un désert nm | *A desert*
Quatre n | *Four*
Un quart nm | *A quarter*
Pâle adj | *Pale*
De la paille nf | *Straw*
Une pince nf | *Pliers*
Ponce (Poncer) v | *To sand*
Une feuille nf | *A leaf*
Une fouille nf | *A search*

MON PREMIER TRAVAIL
MY FIRST JOB

46

What is a Liaison?

A liaison in French is when the final silent consonant of a word is pronounced because the following word begins with a vowel or a silent "h." This helps make the pronunciation of groups of words more fluid.

Here are the three different types of liaisons we will focus on in this exercise:

AUDIO 46.1 🔊

The Z Sound

The **Z sound** happens when the final consonant is an **s** and the next word begins with a vowel or a silent h.

Sans attendre = Sans Zattendre
Without waiting

The T Sound

The **T sound** happens when the final consonant is a **t** and the next word begins with a vowel or a silent h.

Ils vont au parc. = Ils vont Tau parc.
They are going to the park.

The N Sound

The **N sound** happens when the final consonant is a **n** and the next word begins with a vowel or a silent h.

Un emploi = Un Nemploi
A job

AUDIO 46.2 🔊

1. **Écoutez l'audio** et soulignez **les liaisons** comme dans les exemples ci-dessus.
   Listen to the audio and underline the liaisons like in the examples above.

Mon premier travail

J'ai décroché mon premier travail juste après l'université. J'ai passé plusieurs entretiens, et j'étais très enthousiaste à l'idée de commencer à travailler. Après trois entretiens, j'ai eu une offre d'emploi. Le premier jour, je suis arrivé à l'heure au bureau. Mes collègues étaient accueillants et m'ont montré les tâches à réaliser. L'ambiance était agréable et les horaires étaient parfaits pour moi. Après quelques semaines, j'avais déjà appris énormément et je me sentais de plus en plus à l'aise. Mon manager m'a vite donné de nouvelles responsabilités. J'ai travaillé trois ans dans cette entreprise avant de lancer mon propre business.

TRANSLATION

My First Job

I landed my first job right after college. I had several interviews, and I was very excited to start working. After three interviews, I got a job offer. The first day, I arrived at the office on time. My colleagues were welcoming and showed me the tasks to be carried out. The atmosphere was pleasant, and the hours were perfect for me. After a few weeks, I had already learned a lot, and I felt more and more comfortable. My manager quickly gave me new responsibilities. I worked for three years in this company before launching my own business.

AUDIO 46.3 ◄))

VOCABULARY

Un travail nm | *A job*
Premier – Première adj | *First*
Décrocher v | *To land*
Une université nf | *A college*
Passer v | *To have*
Un entretien nm | *An interview*
Enthousiaste adj | *Excited*
Commencer v | *To start*
Travailler v | *To work*
Une offre d'emploi nf | *A job offer*
Un jour nm | *A day*
Arriver v | *To arrive*
Un bureau nm | *An office*
Un – Une collègue n | *A colleague*
Accueillant – Accueillante adj | *Welcoming*
Montrer v | *To show*

Une tâche nf | *A task*
Réaliser v | *To carry out*
L'ambiance nf | *The atmosphere*
Agréable adj | *Pleasant*
Des horaires nm | *Hours*
Parfait – Parfaite adj | *Perfect*
Une semaine nf | *A week*
Apprendre v | *To learn*
Se sentir v | *To feel*
À l'aise adv | *Comfortable*
Un manager nm | *A manager*
Donner v | *To give*
Une responsabilité nf | *A responsibility*
Une entreprise nf | *A company*
Un business nm | *A business*
Propre adj | *Own*

LES LETTRES MUETTES
SILENT LETTERS

47

In this book, we have seen five different French silent letters: **e** in chapter 6, **s** in chapter 16, **t** in chapter 26, **x** in chapter 36, and **d** in chapter 44. Let's do a final exercise that includes all of them! All the silent letters in the following exercise are at the end of the words.

Note: Silent letters and liaisons are different. You can hear a liaison, but it could still be a silent letter.

AUDIO 47.1 ◀))

1. Écoutez ces 20 phrases et **soulignez les lettres muettes e, s, t, x et d**.
   Listen to these 20 sentences and underline the silent letters e, s, t, x, and d.

1.   Il faut être patient dans la vie.

2.   Tu penses qu'ils arriveront à l'heure ?

3.   On boit toujours une tasse de café quand on se lève.

4.   Internet est tellement lent en ce moment !

5.   Tu peux appeler ton client avant de partir ?

6.   J'étudie l'anglais au moins une heure par jour.

7.   Ce meuble est plus grand que je ne le pensais.

8.   La rentrée des classes est en septembre.

9.   Mon mari et moi allons voyager après notre retraite.

10.   Le lac est vide à cause de la sécheresse.

11.   J'ai lu ce livre en deux jours.

12.   C'est bien d'apprendre du nouveau vocabulaire tous les jours.

13.   Elle veut venir avec moi à la piscine dimanche.

14.   Pourquoi est-ce que tu es triste ?

15.   Je n'ai aucune idée de ce qu'elle voulait dire !

16.   Tu auras ton cadeau le jour de ton anniversaire.

17.   Je pense qu'ils sont heureux ensemble.

18.   Il faut porter de la crème solaire pour protéger sa peau.

19.   Les vieilles personnes doivent rester actives au quotidien.

20.   Elle a mal aux dents depuis ce matin.

TRANSLATION

1. *You have to be patient in life.*
2. *Do you think they will arrive on time?*
3. *We always drink a cup of coffee when we get up.*
4. *The internet is so slow right now!*
5. *Can you call your client before leaving?*
6. *I study English at least one hour a day.*
7. *This piece of furniture is bigger than I thought.*
8. *The start of the school year is in September.*
9. *My husband and I are going to travel after we retire.*
10. *The lake is empty because of the drought.*
11. *I read this book in two days.*
12. *It's good to learn new vocabulary every day.*
13. *She wants to come with me to the swimming pool on Sunday.*
14. *Why are you sad?*
15. *I have no idea what she meant!*
16. *You will get your present on your birthday.*
17. *I think they are happy together.*
18. *You should wear sunscreen to protect your skin.*
19. *Old people need to stay active every day.*
20. *She has had a toothache since this morning.*

VOCABULARY

Patient – Patiente adj | *Patient*
La vie nf | *Life*
Penser v | *To think*
Arriver v | *To arrive*
À l'heure | *On time*
Boire v | *To drink*
Toujours adv | *Always*
Une tasse de café nf | *A cup of coffee*
Se lever v | *To get up*
Internet nm | *Internet*
Lent – Lente adj | *Slow*
En ce moment | *Right now*

Appeler v | *To call*
Un client nm | *A client*
Partir v | *To leave*
Étudier v | *To study*
L'anglais nm | *English*
Au moins adv | *At least*
Une heure nf | *An hour*
Un jour nm | *A day*
Un meuble nm | *A piece of furniture*
Grand – Grande adj | *Big*
La rentrée des classes nf | *Start of school*
Septembre nm | *September*

Un mari nm | *A husband*
Voyager v | *To travel*
La retraite nf | *Retirement*
Un lac nm | *A lake*
Vide adj | *Empty*
La sécheresse nf | *Drought*
Un livre nm | *A book*
Apprendre v | *To learn*
Du vocabulaire nm | *Vocabulary*
Nouveau – Nouvelle adj | *New*
Venir v | *To come*
Une piscine nf | *A swimming pool*
Le dimanche nm | *Sunday*
Triste adj | *Sad*
Une idée nf | *An idea*

Un cadeau nm | *A present*
Un anniversaire nm | *A birthday*
Heureux – Heureuse adj | *Happy*
Ensemble adv | *Together*
Porter v | *To wear*
La crème solaire nf | *Sunscreen*
Protéger v | *To protect*
La peau nf | *Skin*
Une personne nf | *A person*
Vieux – Vieille adj | *Old*
Rester v | *To stay*
Actif – Active adj | *Active*
Avoir mal v | *To be in pain*
Une dent nf | *A tooth*
Un matin nm | *A morning*

LES SONS U ET OU
THE SOUNDS U AND OU

48

The sounds **u** and **ou** are often a struggle for French learners. If you have the same issue, it's probably because you can't hear the sound **u**. It's not a common sound in many languages. In this exercise, we will work with **u** and **ou** together to help you differentiate them.

AUDIO 48.1 🔊

u	**Une jupe** nf | *A skirt*
ou	**Un genou** nm | *A knee*

This exercise, "Listen and repeat," is divided into four different parts:

1. The sounds only
2. The sounds in syllables
3. The sounds in words
4. Circle the word you hear

AUDIO 48.2 🔊

1. Écoutez **les sons u et ou** et répétez après moi.
   *Listen to the sounds **u** and **ou** and repeat after me.*

   u – ou

AUDIO 48.3 🔊

2. Écoutez **les sons u et ou** dans **les différentes syllabes** et répétez après moi.
   *Listen to the sounds **u** and **ou** in the different syllables and repeat after me.*

The Sound u

bu – cu – du – fu – ju – lu – mu – nu – pu – ru – su – tu – vu – zu

The Sound ou

bou – cou – dou – fou – jou – lou – mou – nou – pou – rou – sou – tou – vou – zou

3. Écoutez **les différents mots** incluant les sons **u et ou** et répétez après moi.
*Listen to the different words including the sounds **u** and **ou** and repeat after me.*

The Sound u	The Sound ou
Une bulle	L'amour
La culture	Une bouche
Une facture	Courir
Le futur	Court – Courte
Inclure	Un foulard
La lecture	Une fourmi
Des lunettes	Un groupe
Un mur	Nouveau – Nouvelle
Murmurer	Un outil
Une plume	Ouvrir
Réunir	Une poule
Une rupture	Rouge
Une tortue	Une souris
Un virus	Une tour
Une voiture	Tourner

4. Écoutez **l'audio** et **entourez** le mot que je prononce. Chaque mot est répété deux fois.
Listen to the audio and circle the word I say. Each word is repeated twice.

1. Bu – Boue
2. Buche – Bouche
3. Bulle – Boule
4. Du – Doux
5. Jure – Jour
6. Jus – Joue
7. Lu – Loup
8. Nu – Nous
9. Pu – Pou
10. Pull – Poule
11. Rue – Roue
12. Russe – Rousse
13. Su – Sous
14. Sur – Sourd
15. Tu – Tout
16. Vue – Vous

VOCABULARY

L'amour nf | *Love*
La bouche nf | *The mouth*
De la boue nf | *Mud*

Une boule nf | *A ball*
Bu (Boire) v | *Drank (To drink)*
Une buche nf | *A log*

Une bulle nf | *A bubble*
Courir v | *To run*
Court – Courte adj | *Short*
La culture nf | *Culture*
Doux – Douce adj | *Soft*
Du art | *Some*
Une facture nf | *A bill*
Un foulard nm | *A scarf*
Une fourmi nf | *An ant*
Le futur nm | *Future*
Un groupe nm | *A group*
Inclure v | *To include*
Une joue nf | *A cheek*
Un jour nm | *A day*
Jurer v | *To swear*
Du jus nm | *Juice*
La lecture nf | *Reading*
Un loup nm | *A wolf*
Lu (Lire) v | *Read (To read)*
Des lunettes nf | *Glasses*
Un mur nm | *A wall*
Murmurer v | *To whisper*
Nous pr | *We*
Nouveau – Nouvelle adj | *New*
Nu – Nue adj | *Naked*
Un outil nm | *A tool*
Ouvrir v | *To open*

Une plume nf | *A feather*
Une poule nf | *A chicken*
Un pou nm | *A louse*
Le pouvoir nm | *Power*
Un pull nm | *A sweater*
Réunir v | *To reunite*
Une roue nf | *A wheel*
Rouge adj | *Red*
Roux – Rousse adj | *Redhead*
Une rue nf | *A street*
Une rupture nf | *A break up*
Russe adj | *Russian*
Sourd – Sourde adj | *Deaf*
Une souris nf | *A mouse*
Sous prep | *Below*
Su (Savoir) v | *Known (To know)*
Sur prep | *On*
Une tortue nf | *A turtle*
Une tour nf | *A tower*
Tourner v | *To turn*
Tout adj | *All*
Tu pr | *You*
Un virus nm | *A virus*
Une voiture nf | *A car*
Vous pr | *You*
Une vue nf | *A view*

UNE SOIRÉE SANS TÉLÉPHONE
AN EVENING WITHOUT A PHONE

49

AUDIO 49.1 ◄))

1. **Écoutez l'audio** et **lisez l'histoire** en même temps.
   Listen to the audio and read the story at the same time.

Une soirée sans téléphone

Chaque semaine, mon mari et moi essayons de passer une soirée ensemble. Techniquement, on passe toutes nos soirées ensemble mais une fois par semaine, on passe une soirée sans téléphone. Cela nous permet d'être complétement présent, sans distractions. Au début, c'était un peu difficile mais maintenant, on laisse nos téléphones dans un tiroir et on n'y touche pas. Pendant ces soirées, on fait des choses simples mais agréables. Parfois, on joue à des jeux de société, ou on cuisine ensemble un bon repas. De temps en temps, on va au restaurant ou on va boire un verre. C'est tellement bien de ne pas être interrompus par des notifications constantes. Cela nous permet de parler de nos projets et de la vie de tous les jours. On essaye de ne pas parler de travail car on travaille ensemble. On attend toujours avec impatiente notre soirée car on se sent un peu coupés du monde.

TRANSLATION

An Evening without a Phone

Every week, my husband and I try to spend an evening together. Technically, we spend all our evenings together, but once a week, we have a phone-free evening. This allows us to be completely present without distractions. At first, it was a little difficult, but now we leave our phones in a drawer and don't touch them. During these evenings, we do simple but pleasant things. Sometimes, we play board games or cook a nice meal together. From time to time, we go to a restaurant or have a drink. It's so nice not to be interrupted by constant notifications. This allows us to talk about our projects and everyday life. We try not to talk about work because we work together. We always look forward to our evening because we feel cut off from the world.

2. **Écoutez l'audio 49.1** et **numérotez les phrases de 1 à 11 pour les remettre dans l'ordre.**
   Listen to the audio 49.1 and number the sentences from 1 to 11 to put them in order.

Une soirée sans téléphone

– On essaye de ne pas parler de travail car on travaille ensemble.

– Au début, c'était un peu difficile mais maintenant, on laisse nos téléphones dans un tiroir et on n'y touche pas.

– C'est tellement bien de ne pas être interrompus par des notifications constantes.

– Cela nous permet d'être complétement présent, sans distractions.

– Chaque semaine, mon mari et moi essayons de passer une soirée ensemble.

– Pendant ces soirées, on fait des choses simples mais agréables.

– De temps en temps, on va au restaurant ou on va boire un verre.

– On attend toujours avec impatiente notre soirée car on se sent un peu coupés du monde.

– Parfois, on joue à des jeux de société, ou on cuisine ensemble un bon repas.

– Techniquement, on passe toutes nos soirées ensemble mais une fois par semaine, on passe une soirée sans téléphone.

– Cela nous permet de parler de nos projets et de la vie de tous les jours.

AUDIO 49.2))

VOCABULARY

Une soirée nf | *An evening*
Un téléphone nm | *A phone*
Une semaine nf | *A week*
Un mari nm | *A husband*
Passer v | *To spend*
Ensemble adv | *Together*
Permettre v | *To allow*
Être présent – présente v | *To be present*
Une distraction nf | *A distraction*
Laisser v | *To leave*
Un tiroir nm | *A drawer*
Toucher v | *To touch*
Simple adj | *Simple*
Agréable adj | *Pleasant*
Jouer v | *To play*
Un jeu de société nm | *A board game*

Cuisiner v | *To cook*
Un bon repas adj + nm | *A good meal*
Un restaurant nm | *A restaurant*
Boire un verre | *To have a drink*
Être interrompu – interrompue v |
To be interrupted
Une notification nf | *A notification*
Constant – Constante adj | *Constant*
Un projet nm | *A project*
La vie de tous les jours nf | *Everyday life*
Parler v | *To talk*
Le travail nm | *Work*
Travailler v | *To work*
Attendre avec impatiente | *To look forward to*
Se sentir coupé v | *To feel cut off*
Le monde nm | *The world*

LE JOUR OÙ ON A PLANTÉ UN ARBRE
THE DAY WE PLANTED A TREE

50

AUDIO 50.1 🔊

1. **Écoutez l'audio** et **lisez l'histoire** en même temps.
   Listen to the audio and read the story at the same time.

Le jour où on a planté un arbre

Le village où j'ai grandi se trouve au milieu d'une forêt. Cela ressemble à un paysage de carte postale. Il y a une rivière qui traverse le village. Il y a toujours des enfants qui s'y baignent quand il fait chaud. À chaque fois que je retourne au village, je me promène au bord de cette rivière. À la fin du sentier, il y a un arbre qu'on a planté quand j'étais à l'école. Je devais avoir 10 ans je pense. C'est un de mes meilleurs souvenirs. Cette année-là, on avait appris plein de choses sur les arbres et les animaux. Notre professeur nous avait montré comment reconnaître les différents arbres par leurs feuilles et les animaux par leurs empreintes. Je me souviens encore de mon livre avec les feuilles mortes collées sur chaque page. À la fin de l'année, notre classe a planté un arbre. C'était une vraie aventure à l'époque. Aujourd'hui, l'arbre a bien poussé. Il y a aussi une plaque avec le nom de notre classe et l'année où on l'a planté. C'est vraiment un bon souvenir.

TRANSLATION

The Day we Planted a Tree

The village where I grew up is in the middle of a forest. It looks like a postcard landscape. There is a river that runs through the village. There are always children swimming there when it is hot. Every time I return to the village, I walk by the river. At the end of the trail, there is a tree that we planted when I was at school. I must have been ten years old, I think. It's one of my best memories. That year, we learned a lot about trees and animals. Our teacher showed us how to recognize different trees by their leaves and animals by their footprints. I still remember my book with the dead leaves glued to each page. At the end of the year, our class planted a tree. It was a real adventure at the time. Today, the tree has grown well. There is also a plaque with the name of our class and the year we planted it. It's really a good memory.

Le jour on a planté un arbre

Le village où j'ai grandi se trouve au milieu d'une _____ . Cela ressemble à un paysage de carte postale. Il y a une _____ qui traverse le village. Il y a toujours des enfants qui s'y baignent quand il fait _____ . À chaque fois que je retourne au village, je me promène au bord de cette rivière. À la fin du sentier, il y a un _____ qu'on a planté quand j'étais à l'école. Je devais avoir 10 _____ je pense. C'est un de mes meilleurs _____ . Cette année-là, on avait appris plein de choses sur les arbres et les _____ . Notre professeur nous avait montré comment reconnaître les différents arbres par leurs feuilles et les animaux par leurs empreintes. Je me souviens encore de mon _____ avec les feuilles mortes collées sur chaque _____ . À la fin de l'année, notre classe a planté un arbre. C'était une vraie _____ à l'époque. Aujourd'hui, l'arbre a bien poussé. Il y a aussi une _____ avec le nom de notre classe et l'année où on l'a planté. C'est vraiment un _____ souvenir.

AUDIO 50.2 ◄)）

VOCABULARY

Le jour nm | *The day*	**Un meilleur souvenir** adj + nm | *A best memory*
Planter v | *To plant*	**Apprendre** v | *To learn*
Un arbre nm | *A tree*	**Un animal – Des animaux** nm |
Un village nm | *A village*	*An animal – Animals*
Grandir v | *To grow up*	**Un professeur** nm | *A teacher*
Se trouver v | *To be (located)*	**Reconnaître** v | *To recognize*
Au milieu de adv | *In the middle of*	**Différent – Différente** adj | *Different*
Une forêt nf | *A forest*	**Une feuille** nf | *A leaf*
Ressembler v | *To look like*	**Une empreinte** nf | *A footprint*
Un paysage nm | *A landscape*	**Se souvenir** v | *To remember*
Une carte postale nf | *A postcard*	**Un livre** nm | *A book*
Une rivière nf | *A river*	**Une feuille morte** nf + adj | *A dead leaf*
Traverser v | *To run through*	**Coller** v | *To glue*
Un enfant nm | *A child*	**Une page** nf | *A page*
Se baigner v | *To swim*	**Une classe** nf | *A class*
Faire chaud v | *To be hot*	**Une vraie aventure** adj + nf | *A real adventure*
Retourner v | *To return*	**Pousser** v | *To grow*
Se promener v | *To walk by*	**Une plaque** nf | *A plaque*
Un sentier nm | *A trail*	**Un nom** nm | *A name*
Une école nf | *A school*	**Une année** nf | *A year*

ANSWER KEY

CHAPTER 1

Mes amis viennent dîner

Ce soir, mes amis viennent dîner chez **moi**. On est quatre en tout. Une fois par mois, un de nous reçoit les autres pour un **repas** simple. C'est une bonne façon de passer du temps **ensemble**. Ce n'est pas beaucoup de **travail** vu que c'est une fois tous les quatre mois. Cette fois-ci, je prépare une lasagne avec les **tomates** de mon jardin. J'ai aussi fait du pain ce matin pour faire du pain à l'ail. Il est déjà prêt, je n'ai plus qu'à le mettre au **four** avant de servir. C'est la première fois que je fais une lasagne mais elle a l'air très bonne. Pour l'apéritif, j'ai prévu une **bouteille** de champagne et des amuse-bouches. En dessert, ça sera un bol de glace avec des **fraises** et des framboises. Même si on fait toujours un repas simple, cela prend quand même toute la journée à **préparer**. Il faut ranger, nettoyer, préparer le repas et mettre la **table**. Encore heureux qu'on est que quatre car dans mon petit **appartement**, j'ai seulement assez de place pour une table de quatre personnes. Mes amis arriveront dans une **heure** donc je dois aller me préparer pour être à l'heure.

1. Atteindre
2. Brun
3. Un cintre
4. Un copain
5. Un coussin
6. Un dessin
7. La fin
8. Un frein
9. Un grain
10. Impossible
11. Un jardin
12. Un magasin
13. Une main
14. Un matin
15. Plein
16. Un poussin
17. Simple
18. Teindre
19. Du vin
20. Un voisin

La tempête de neige

7 – C'est la première tempête de neige cette année.
2 – Il n'est que 18 heures mais les habitants sont déjà chez eux.
9 – L'hiver peut maintenant commencer.
3 – Il n'y a personne dans les rues et pas de voiture sur la route.
6 – Apparemment, il va tomber plus d'un mètre de neige en quelques heures.
4 – La météo prévoit une tempête de neige ce soir.

1 – Tout est calme dans le petit village de Mégève.

8 – Les pelles à neige sont prêtes et les déneigeuses attendent impatiemment dans les garages.

5 – Mégève est un village en montagne donc les habitants sont habitués aux tempêtes de neige.

CHAPTER 4

1. Une banque
2. Blanche
3. Un champion
4. Décembre
5. Dedans
6. Une dent
7. Emporter
8. Un enfant
9. Un fantôme
10. Grand
11. Une jambe
12. Un jambon
13. Manger
14. Un manteau
15. Un pantalon
16. Penser
17. Le printemps
18. Rentrer
19. Un serpent
20. Le vent

CHAPTER 5

1. ~~Poisson~~ – Poison
2. ~~Bougie~~ – Bouger
3. Chaud – ~~Chaude~~
4. ~~Cacher~~ – Casser
5. Port – ~~Porte~~
6. Plage – ~~Page~~
7. ~~Chanter~~ – Enchanté
8. Chasse – ~~Chasser~~
9. Livre – ~~Libre~~
10. ~~Poule~~ – Pôle
11. ~~Chapeau~~ – Château
12. Brun – ~~Brune~~
13. Feu – ~~Fou~~
14. ~~Fille~~ – File
15. Visse – ~~Fils~~
16. ~~Gare~~ – Guerre
17. Cou – ~~Coule~~
18. Carte – ~~Quart~~
19. ~~Blanc~~ – Blé
20. Pont – ~~Ponce~~

CHAPTER 6

1. Elle veut prendre de meilleures habitudes.
2. L'herbe n'arrête pas de pousser ces dernières semaines !
3. Tu es encore jeune pour choisir.
4. Éteins la télévision si tu quittes la pièce.
5. Je ne pense pas qu'elle soit jalouse.
6. Ce pull est trop large pour moi.
7. Il est tout le temps malade.
8. Fais attention à la marche.
9. Rien de mieux qu'une balade dans la nature.
10. Je mange souvent une banane à 4 heures.
11. C'est nécessaire d'être bien préparer.

12. Il **neige** depuis ce matin.
13. On **plante** des **carottes chaque année**.
14. J'ai perdu la **page** de mon **livre**.
15. N'**oublie** pas ton **écharpe**.
16. Il y a toujours des travaux sur l'**autoroute**.
17. Est-ce que tu as le temps de **prendre** un café ?
18. J'aime bien le lait de soja mais je **préfère** le lait d'**amandes**.
19. C'est mon **anniversaire** dans **une semaine**.
20. On **loue** toujours **une voiture** quand on **voyage**.

CHAPTER 7

Les traboules de Lyon

Est-ce que vous savez qu'il y a des **passages** secrets dans la ville de Lyon ? Ces passages secrets s'appellent des traboules. Ce sont des passages qui relient deux **rues** à travers des maisons ou des immeubles. Elles existent depuis la Renaissance mais certaines sont plus récentes, du 18 et 19eme **siècles**. En gros, c'est un raccourci. Les **habitants** de Lyon les utilisent tous les jours et les **touristes** adorent les découvrir. Il y a plus de 500 traboules mais beaucoup d'entre elles sont fermées pour les **préserver**. Aujourd'hui, on peut encore en visiter 80. Les propriétaires peuvent décider de les fermer si les **visiteurs** posent des problèmes aux habitants du quartier. Si vous voulez **découvrir** les traboules, la meilleure façon c'est de prendre un guide. Un guide peut vous montrer toutes les traboules qui sont encore accessibles au **public**. Les visites sont en général pleines d'anecdotes et d'informations qui sont difficiles à **trouver**. Quand on visite une traboule, il faut être silencieux. Le bruit résonne dans les **maisons** et les immeubles. Il faut aussi les laisser comme on les a trouvées ; propres et sans **trace** de notre passage.

CHAPTER 8

1. **Un bon**
2. **Un canon**
3. **Un cochon**
4. **Un combat**
5. **Complet**
6. **Fonder**
7. **Long**
8. **Un menton**
9. **Une montre**
10. **Un oncle**
11. **Une opinion**
12. **Pardon**
13. **Un pigeon**
14. **Une potion**
15. **Une prison**
16. **Une réunion**
17. **Une question**
18. **Une saison**
19. **Un son**
20. **Un talon**

CHAPTER 9

Le bus n'est pas passé

14 – Elle va devoir appeler un taxi si elle veut arriver à l'heure au travail !

3 – Arrivée dans la cuisine, elle prépare son petit déjeuner.

9 – Elle arrive toujours à la même heure et le bus est rarement en retard.

11 – Sarah attend et attend mais son bus n'arrive pas.

5 – Une fois son petit déjeuner fini, elle va se brosser les dents et se maquiller.

7 – Elle arrive à l'arrêt de bus vers 7h10.

1 – Ce matin commence comme tous les autres matins pour Sarah.

8 – Le bus arrive normalement à 7h15.

10 – Cinq minutes à attendre ce n'est pas beaucoup.

6 – À 7 heures, elle part de la maison pour prendre son bus pour aller au travail.

2 – Elle se réveille à 6 heures, s'habille avant de quitter sa chambre et descend pour manger.

12 – Il est bientôt 7h30 et rien !

4 – Elle mange la même chose tous les jours : deux tranches de pain avec de la confiture et un peu de beurre et une tasse de café.

13 – Son bus n'est pas passé.

CHAPTER 10

Une semaine à la montagne

1. Qui doit encore faire sa valise ? Camille
2. Qui a perdu son passeport ? Camille
3. Qui doit encore laver quelques habits ? Steve
4. Qui doit acheter des barres protéinées ? Steve
5. Qui a reçu ses nouvelles chaussures de marche ? Steve
6. Qui propose de faire du shopping près de l'hôtel ? Camille
7. Qui dit de se rejoindre à neuf heures à l'aéroport ? Steve
8. Qui va écrire à l'autre avant de partir ? Camille

CHAPTER 11

La cabane dans le jardin

Dans le jardin de mes **parents**, il y a une vieille cabane. C'est une cabane en bois avec un toit en **métal**. Avec mes frères, on y jouait souvent quand on était petits. Elle semblait énorme quand on y jouait mais maintenant que je suis **adulte**, elle a l'air minuscule. Je suis un peu **nostalgique** car mes parents vont la détruire bientôt. Ils disent qu'elle est en mauvais état et qu'ils ne s'en servent pas. C'est **vrai** qu'elle est vide. Il n'y a rien à l'intérieur. Les **tempêtes** de l'année dernière ont abimé la **porte** et les fenêtres. Mes parents disent que ce n'est pas la peine de la **réparer**. Ils disent que cela coûterait trop cher. Je suis d'accord avec eux mais je suis un peu **triste** qu'elle soit démolie. Je pense que je vais garder quelques planches. Peut-être que je les utiliserai pour faire un meuble, un plateau, ou peut-être juste un **cadre**. Ça sera une chouette façon de garder un **souvenir** de notre cabane.

CHAPTER 12

1. Je dois me changer avant de partir.
2. **On** habite à la montagne.
3. Le salon de coiffure sera fermé ce dimanche.
4. **On** peut manger maintenant si tu as faim.
5. Ma fille a rendez-vous chez le dentiste lundi prochain.
6. Le temps est frais en automne.
7. J'aime prendre un bain quand j'ai froid.
8. C'est impossible de résoudre ce problème.
9. Beaucoup préfère le vin blanc au vin rouge.
10. Il y a plein de dessins accrochés au frigo.
11. J'ai peint ma chambre en blanc.
12. Est-ce que tu peux baisser le son ?
13. Les pigeons attendent de recevoir du pain.
14. Mon oncle ne sera pas là à notre mariage.
15. Le client a rempli le contrat.

CHAPTER 13

Ma journée de congé

11 – Une journée bien remplie, pour moi, c'est toujours une bonne journée.

7 – Quand je rentre, je mets les draps et les serviettes dans le sèche-linge et je range les courses.

1 – J'aime être productif pendant ma journée de congé.

6 – Sur le chemin du retour, je m'arrête à la pompe à essence pour faire le plein.

3 – Je lave aussi les draps de lit et les serviettes de bain.

5 – Une fois que j'ai fait ma liste de courses, je vais au magasin pour faire mes courses.

4 – Pendant que la machine à laver fait son travail, je regarde ce que j'ai dans le frigo et les placards de la cuisine pour les repas de la semaine.

9 – Si j'ai faim, je prépare le dîner, sinon, je lis un bon livre pendant une heure ou deux.

2 – Je commence souvent par faire un peu de rangement et un peu de ménage.

10 – Si je ne suis pas productif, j'ai l'impression de perdre mon temps.

8 – Après ça, je fais une heure de sport avant de me doucher.

CHAPTER 14

Un millefeuille

Un portefeuille

Un fauteuil

Un accueil

Un écureuil

Un œil

Accueillir

Un chevreuil

Cueillir

Le deuil

L'orgueil

Un cercueil

Une feuille

Le seuil

CHAPTER 15

1. Ventre – ~~Vendre~~
2. ~~Note~~ – Notre
3. Fleur – ~~Peur~~
4. ~~Pour~~ – Pur
5. ~~Peau~~ – Peu
6. ~~Roule~~ – Rouge
7. Gros – ~~Gras~~
8. ~~Marche~~ – Marché
9. ~~Banc~~ – Blanc
10. Lu – ~~Loup~~
11. Moi – ~~Moine~~
12. ~~Bois~~ – Boîte
13. Faux – ~~Feu~~
14. Attendre – ~~Entendre~~
15. ~~Sol~~ – Sale
16. Nous – ~~Nu~~
17. ~~Bague~~ – Blague
18. Bras – ~~Bas~~
19. ~~Brise~~ – Bise
20. Courir – ~~Nourrir~~

CHAPTER 16

1. Le **mois** de février a 28 **jours**.
2. Le **repas** sera servi dans deux **heures**.
3. Il s'est fait mal au **dos** en déplaçant ces **boîtes**.
4. Le **bois** derrière chez moi me fait **toujours** peur.
5. Mon **colis** devrait être livré ce matin.
6. Je n'ai **jamais** vu ce film.
7. Cela vaut **moins** que cent **euros**.
8. Qu'est-ce que tu **fais** ce soir ?
9. Je **dors** souvent tard le samedi.
10. Le ciel est **gris** aujourd'hui.
11. Apprendre le **français** peut être difficile.
12. Ce documentaire est **très** intéressant.

13. Je viendrai au **repas sans** mon mari.
14. Tes **dessins** sont vraiment **jolis**.
15. Les **jours** sont **courts** en hiver.
16. Il fait **mauvais depuis** une semaine.
17. Je trie mes **habits** en hiver et en été.
18. Il n'y a **plus** de pain chez le boulanger.
19. Mon chien a des **taches brunes** sur le **corps**.
20. **Ils** n'ont **pas** besoin d'être **présents** à la réunion.

CHAPTER 17

Le marché du dimanche

Dans le petit **village** de Valmont-aux-Bois, il y a un marché tous les dimanches **matin**. C'est un marché en plein air, dans les **rues** de la vieille ville. Une cinquantaine de vendeurs viennent de toute la **province** pour vendre leurs produits. Ils arrivent tôt pour avoir les meilleures **places**. Certains arrivent à 5 heures du matin. Ils s'installent et commencent à décharger leur **camion** directement. Il y a beaucoup de **choses** à faire avant que les premiers clients arrivent à 7 heures. Techniquement, il n'y a pas d'heure d'ouverture mais c'est rare que les gens arrivent avant 7 heures. On peut tout acheter au marché : des fruits, des **légumes**, des épices, de la viande, du poisson, des œufs, des **fleurs**, des habits et même de la décoration pour la **maison**. Les clients sont souvent les mêmes et ils achètent presque toujours la même chose. Quand il fait **beau**, c'est un vrai plaisir de se promener dans les rues en faisant ses courses. Quand il pleut par contre, ce n'est pas très gai. Même les vendeurs savent qu'ils vendront moins si le **temps** n'est pas bon.

CHAPTER 18

1. Une abeille
2. Une bouteille
3. Conseiller
4. Une corbeille
5. Merveilleux
6. Un oreiller
7. Pareil
8. Se réveiller
9. Le soleil
10. Surveiller

CHAPTER 19

La fête d'anniversaire de mon fils

12 – Je devrais avoir assez de temps pour tout faire.
5 – Je vais d'abord aller chercher son gâteau que j'ai commandé à la boulangerie.
1 – Aujourd'hui, c'est l'anniversaire de mon fils.

11 – La dernière chose à faire après tout ça, c'est d'emballer ses cadeaux.

9 – Je vais mettre deux tables près du château gonflable.

3 – Tous ses amis arriveront dans quelques heures pour la fête qu'on a organisée.

13 – J'espère juste que personne ne sera malade dans le château gonflable car il y a beaucoup à manger !

2 – Il a sept ans.

7 – Une fois rentrée, je dois accrocher les banderoles et mettre la table.

10 – La première avec des chips et des petites choses à grignoter et la deuxième avec des boissons.

8 – Un château gonflable sera livré dans deux heures et installé dans le jardin.

4 – Je dois me dépêcher pour tout faire.

6 – J'ai oublié d'acheter des bougies donc je dois aller en acheter au magasin.

CHAPTER 20

Une journée au zoo

Nos enfants adorent aller au zoo. **Ils aiment** admirer **les animaux**. Ils peuvent passer **des heures** à regarder **les éléphants** et **les ours**. Ils sont toujours contents de **les observer** pendant qu'ils mangent, qu'ils dorment, ou qu'ils se promènent dans **leurs enclos**. Mais au zoo, il n'y a pas que les gros mammifères, il y a aussi **les oiseaux**, les reptiles et les poissons. Les cages **des oiseaux sont immenses** et **les aquariums** sont plein de couleurs vives. Avec tous **les animaux** qu'il y a à voir, une journée au zoo passe toujours trop vite. **Les enfants** ont toujours hâte d'y retourner.

CHAPTER 21

Un nouveau camping-car

J'adore faire du camping mais je déteste **dormir** en tente. Dormir sur un **matelas** gonflable, ce n'est jamais confortable. Sans parler des **animaux** qui vivent autour des campings. Cette année, on a décidé d'acheter un camping-car. Je pense que je me sentirais mieux si je dormais à l'intérieur au lieu de dans une tente. C'est cher mais on fait du camping au moins dix **fois** par an donc ça en vaut la peine. Cela fait un peu plus de trois **mois** qu'on regarde les petites annonces tous les jours, mais **rien**. Personne ne vend un camping-car au milieu de l'**hiver**. Maintenant que c'est le **printemps**, on voit de plus en plus d'annonces chaque jour mais ce n'est jamais ce qu'on cherche. Mais ce matin, tout a changé. Je prenais mon **café** en regardant les petites annonces sur mon ordinateur quand je l'ai vu ; le camping-car de nos **rêves** ! Il a seulement cinq ans et il a très peu de **kilomètres** au compteur. La personne qui le vend habite seulement à dix kilomètres de chez nous ! On va le voir cet après-midi mais je pense que c'est le **bon**. Le prix est parfait et j'ai hâte de ne plus dormir en tente.

CHAPTER 22

1. L'ail
2. Une bataille
3. Un détail
4. Un épouvantail
5. Un maillot

6. Une médaille
7. Une paille
8. Le rail
9. Tailler
10. Travailler

CHAPTER 23

Une machine à pain

5 – On choisit les options et la machine pétrit le pain et le cuit en quelques heures.

9 – Une fois bien levée, il fallait la pétrir de nouveau.

10 – En plus du travail, c'était aussi très salissant.

3 – La seule chose qu'on doit faire, c'est d'y mettre tous les ingrédients.

12 – Je ne ferai plus jamais mon pain à la main maintenant que j'ai une machine à pain !

4 – On commence par l'eau, puis la farine et le sel, avant d'ajouter la levure en dernier.

7 – Il fallait mélanger les ingrédients et puis pétrir la pâte pendant une dizaine de minutes.

2 – La machine fait tout pour nous.

6 – Avant ça, on faisait notre pain à la main et c'était toujours beaucoup de travail.

8 – La pâte devait reposer pendant deux heures.

1 – On vient d'acheter une machine à pain et je n'arrive pas à croire qu'on n'en ait pas acheté une avant !

11 – Il y avait toujours de la farine partout et de la pâte collée sur le plan de travail.

CHAPTER 24

Le marché de Noël

Tous **les ans**, la ville organise **un incroyable** marché de Noël au mois de décembre. Il ouvre ses portes le 1er décembre. Les visiteurs viennent de toute la France pour faire **des achats**, déguster du vin chaud, et s'imprégner de l'ambiance de Noël. Beaucoup de vendeurs sont **des artistes**. Ils fabriquent eux-mêmes les décorations, les jouets et les **produits artisanaux** qu'ils vendent. **Les enfants**, eux, sont là pour les chocolats chauds et le sapin géant au milieu du marché. **Les odeurs** de vin chaud et de pain d'épices, ainsi que les musiques de Noël remplissent les rues de la ville. Chaque année, **c'est un** succès pour les petits et les grands.

CHAPTER 25

1. ~~Surpris~~ – Surprise
2. ~~Jaune~~ – Jeune
3. Café – ~~Carré~~
4. ~~Cabane~~ – Cabine
5. Balle – ~~Boule~~
6. Pousser – ~~Passer~~
7. ~~Rouge~~ – Rage
8. Goût – ~~Goutte~~
9. ~~Rêve~~ – Rive
10. ~~Lieu~~ – Vieux
11. Talon – ~~Talent~~
12. ~~Roman~~ – Romain
13. Lever – ~~Laver~~
14. Payer – ~~Pays~~
15. ~~Vue~~ – Vie
16. Banc – ~~Bon~~
17. ~~Prendre~~ – Pendre
18. ~~Feu~~ – Fou
19. Prêt – ~~Prête~~
20. ~~Casier~~ – Caissier

CHAPTER 26

1. Elles n'**aiment** pas le **chocolat** blanc.
2. C'est un **objet** bizarre.
3. Il a beaucoup de **talent**.
4. Le professeur sera **absent** ce vendredi.
5. Mon mari est un homme **galant**.
6. Le **chat dort** devant le feu **ouvert**.
7. Il y a eu un **accident** près de chez moi la **nuit** dernière.
8. Les Français **mangent** des **escargots**.
9. Il ne **fait** jamais attention à ses affaires.
10. Ce **bâtiment** va être démoli au mois de **juillet**.
11. Notre séjour **était parfait** !
12. Mes **parents** se **reposent** dans le salon.
13. Il y a beaucoup d'**accents** sur les lettres en français.
14. Est-ce que tu es **prêt** ?
15. Notre chien est plus **petit** que le tien.
16. Tu veux aller au **restaurant** avant ou après le cinéma ?
17. Le **résultat** des élections sera connu demain.
18. J'aurai fini le **rapport** demain.
19. Les **habitants** du village **organisent** un marché de Noël chaque année.
20. Il **faut** se concentrer sur le **présent**.

CHAPTER 27

Qu'est-ce que j'ai dans mon sac ?

J'ai beaucoup de **choses** dans mon sac, beaucoup trop de choses je **pense**. J'ai mon portefeuille avec mes **documents** d'identités et mes cartes bancaires. J'ai les clés de mon appartement, de ma **voiture** et les clés de mon bureau. J'ai mon **téléphone** bien sûr, parfois j'ai aussi son chargeur si je n'ai plus de **batterie**. J'ai quelques produits de beauté comme du beurre de cacao et de la **crème** pour les mains ainsi qu'une petite bouteille de désinfectant pour les mains. Ça c'est l'essentiel. Pour le **reste**, j'ai aussi un stylo, un petit cahier, un **paquet** de mouchoirs et un sac réutilisable pour faire mes **courses**. Le plus compliqué, c'est quand je **change** de sac. Je dois tout vider et décider ce que je **garde** ou pas.

CHAPTER 28

1.	Briller	6.	Gentille
2.	Une chenille	7.	Une grille
3.	Une coquille	8.	Griller
4.	La famille	9.	Une quille
5.	Une fille	10.	La vanille

CHAPTER 29

Ma première tasse de café

5 – Je ne trouvais pas ça très bon mais je voulais faire comme tout le monde.

2 – Le plus souvent, c'était mon père qui remplissant la machine et y ajoutait du café moulu.

4 – Quand j'avais plus ou moins dix ans, je buvais quelques gorgées ici et là.

1 – Je ne me souviens pas exactement de la première fois que j'ai goûté du café mais mes parents en préparaient une cruche tous les matins.

8 – Pour me réchauffer, il m'a donné une tasse de café avec beaucoup de crème et de sucre.

6 – La première fois que j'ai bu une tasse de café complète, c'était au camping avec mon père.

9 – Je me souviens que cela m'a réchauffé immédiatement.

7 – Il faisait froid et mon père avait oublié d'apporter du chocolat chaud.

10 – Maintenant que je suis plus âgé, je bois une ou deux tasses de café le matin mais je le bois toujours noir, sans sucre et sans crème.

3 – Cela sentait toujours bon le café quand je me levais.

CHAPTER 30

Bientôt à la retraite

1.	Qui part à la retraite à la fin du mois ?	Steve
2.	Qui est déjà à la retraite depuis bientôt deux ans ?	Camille
3.	Qui était responsable d'un gros projet ?	Steve
4.	Qui avait un mari déjà à la retraite ?	Camille

5.	Qui a des horaires plus flexibles ?	Steve
6.	Qui rénove sa maison ?	Camille
7.	Qui veut voyager ?	Steve
8.	Qui ne touche pas sa pension complète ?	Camille
9.	Qui a une réunion ?	Steve

CHAPTER 31

Les coupures de courant

La météo où j'habite peut être un peu **difficile**. Ce n'est pas seulement où j'habite, c'est dans toute la **région**. On a toujours beaucoup de vent, surtout en **automne**. Le vent peut aller jusqu'à 100 km/h. C'est souvent le sujet de **conversation** préféré au magasin ou au **café**. À cause du vent, on a beaucoup de coupures de courant. Ce n'est pas très **grave** mais c'est toujours embêtant si on n'est pas **préparé**. On fait toujours attention à la météo mais parfois le **vent** semble arriver de nulle part. J'ai acheté une grosse **batterie** portable pour charger nos téléphones ou nos **ordinateurs** portables. Quand une coupure de courant dure plus d'une journée, il faut utiliser un générateur pour ne pas perdre toute la **nourriture** dans le frigo et le congélateur. Ce n'est pas la fin du **monde** mais il faut toujours être préparé.

1.	Bouillir	6.	Une grenouille
2.	Du bouillon	7.	Des nouilles
3.	Une citrouille	8.	Une ratatouille
4.	Le fenouil	9.	Rouiller
5.	Gazouiller	10.	La trouille

Une visite au musée

3   – Je ne travaille jamais le lundi donc je suis libre toute la journée.

9   – On va voir de vieilles locomotives et comment elles fonctionnaient à l'époque.

2   – Son professeur m'a demandé de les accompagner et j'ai accepté.

5   – Deux autres parents seront avec nous, donc on sera 4 adultes au total.

11   – Le musée vient d'ajouter des activités interactives donc les enfants seront bien occupés pendant toute la visite.

6   – Chaque adulte sera responsable d'un groupe de 5 enfants.

10   – Ça sera très intéressant pour les enfants vu qu'il y a beaucoup de trains qui passent dans la ville.

1   –   La classe de ma fille va visiter un musée aujourd'hui.
4   –   On doit être à l'école vers 7 heures et demie pour organiser la journée.
7   –   Le budget de l'école est limité donc on va prendre les transports en commun.
8   –   Le musée qu'ils ont choisi cette année est le musée des trains.

CHAPTER 34

Une promenade en forêt

Louis et **son adorable** petit chien **sont en** train de se promener dans la forêt. La forêt **est à** quelques minutes de sa maison. Il n'a même pas besoin de conduire pour leurs promenades quotidiennes. Cette forêt **est incroyable**. **Les arbres sont immenses** et il y a plein d'oiseaux qui chantent. Après quelques minutes de marche, Louis aperçoit quelque chose qui bouge au loin. **C'est un** petit groupe de cerfs. **Les animaux** le regardent pendant **un instant** avant de disparaître dans les bois. Encore heureux que son chien ne **les a** pas vus ! **C'est une** journée parfaite pour une longue balade.

CHAPTER 35

1. Garde – Gourde
2. Dessus – Dessous
3. Court – Pour
4. Actif – Active
5. Adopter – Adapter
6. Savoir – Saveur
7. Amener – Emmener

8. Accent – Accès
9. Achat – Chat
10. Rue – Roue
11. Chiant – Chien
12. Long – Lent
13. Ton – Temps
14. Son – Sans

15. Peur – Pour
16. Pull – Poule
17. Mousse – Mouche
18. Sel – Seul
19. Plat – Plan
20. Poivre – Pauvre

CHAPTER 36

1. Le **prix** de ce lit est beaucoup trop cher.
2. Ce que tu dis est **faux**.
3. La **croix** est tombée pendant la nuit.
4. Les **bijoux** de ma mère ont disparu.
5. Les **Jeux** Olympiques se sont déroulés à Paris.
6. Tous les **feux** de la ville sont en panne.
7. Mon chien devient **vieux**.
8. J'ai les **cheveux** longs depuis toujours.
9. Il est tellement **heureux** depuis qu'il a changé de travail.
10. Mes **deux** frères sont célibataires.
11. C'est **généreux** de ta part.

12. Il est **nerveu<u>x</u>** de parler en public.
13. Les **eau<u>x</u>** usées ne sont pas bien traitées.
14. Tu es **sérieu<u>x</u>** ?
15. Je n'ai pas le **choi<u>x</u>**.
16. Mon **épou<u>x</u>** sera présent à la réunion.
17. Je mange des **noi<u>x</u>** tous les jours.
18. Ce coussin est vraiment **dou<u>x</u>**.
19. Qu'est-ce que tu **veu<u>x</u>** faire aujourd'hui ?
20. Mon mari a les **cheveu<u>x</u> rou<u>x</u>**.

CHAPTER 37

L'incident au supermarché

Il y a quelques **jours**, j'étais au supermarché et j'ai renversé une **pile** de boîtes de conserve. Je n'arrive toujours pas à y **croire**. J'ai vraiment honte. Je marchais devant les **frigos** quand une personne avec un caddie est arrivée de l'autre côté. J'ai fait quelques **pas** en arrière pour lui laisser assez de **place** pour passer. Je n'ai pas fait attention à ce qu'il y avait derrière **moi**. Quand j'ai senti quelque chose contre mon **dos**, c'était déjà trop tard. J'ai reculé dans une **grande** pile de boîtes de conserve parfaitement empilées. Elles sont tombées et ont roulé dans toutes les **directions**. Tout le monde me regardait. J'étais tellement gênée ! Un **employé** du magasin est arrivé en moins d'une minute. Il m'a rassuré que cela arrivait **souvent**. Il commencé à ramasser les boîtes de conserve mais certaines étaient trop abîmées. Je voulais les **acheter** mais il a dit que ce n'était pas nécessaire. Je suis gênée que d'y **repenser**.

CHAPTER 38

1. Les **feuille**s commencent à changer de couleur.
2. La gren**ouille** saute dans l'étang.
3. Je trav**aille** sur mon projet avec ma collègue.
4. Le pap**illon** s'est posé sur la chaise de jardin.
5. Ma **fille** adore la glace à la van**ille**.
6. Le fermier donne de la p**aille** aux chevaux.
7. J'ai quelque chose dans l'**œil**.
8. Toute ma fam**ille** se réunit pour fêter Noël.
9. Est-ce que tu as vu ma bout**eille** d'eau ?
10. On a un plat de n**ouille**s pour le déjeuner.
11. Le jardinier t**aille** les arbres du parc.
12. L'ab**eille** va de fleur en fleur.
13. Je vais c**ueil**lir des fraises dans le jardin.

14. On se rév**eille** vers 7 heures tous les matins.
15. Mon or**eille** me fait un peu mal aujourd'hui.
16. Le gagnant a reçu une méd**aille** d'or.
17. Il s'hab**ille** rapidement pour aller à l'école.
18. J'adore la ratat**ouille** !
19. Le sol**eil** br**ille** dans le ciel.
20. Ajoute un peu d'**ail** pour plus de saveur.

CHAPTER 39

Le marathon

5 – Il a gagné plusieurs courses de 10 et 20 kilomètres mais il n'a jamais couru aussi longtemps.

1 – Mon frère est très athlétique.

4 – Un marathon fait 42 kilomètres donc c'est définitivement un exploit sportif.

10 – Il est vraiment motivé !

2 – Il court presque tous les jours.

6 – Il s'entraîne beaucoup pour être prêt.

9 – Il mange beaucoup de légumes et de protéines.

13 – On a tous hâte de le voir franchir la ligne d'arrivée.

7 – Chaque semaine, il court de plus en plus longtemps pour améliorer son endurance.

11 – Toute la famille le soutient et on sera tous là le jour de la course pour l'encourager.

8 – En plus de ça, il fait aussi attention à son alimentation.

12 – Le grand jour est dans deux mois.

3 – Son prochain objectif est de courir un marathon.

CHAPTER 40

Un voyage en train

Cet après-midi, **mon amie** et moi avons pris le train pour aller à la mer. **On est** arrivées vers treize heures. Le voyage en train n'a pris qu'une heure et n'a coûté que **trois euros**. Cela en vaut vraiment la peine. On compte trouver **un hôtel** pour rester jusque demain. Il fait trop froid pour nager mais **on aime** beaucoup marcher. La plage **est interminable** donc on peut marcher pendant **des heures**. Vers **dix-sept heures**, on va certainement aller prendre un café et chercher un restaurant pour le dîner. **On a** envie de manger italien, probablement des pâtes ou des pizzas.

CHAPTER 41

Les urgences

Je suis aux urgences car je me suis foulé la **cheville**. C'était un accident vraiment **bête**. Pour accéder à mon **jardin**, je dois descendre quelques **marches**. Ce matin, alors que je portais un panier de linge, mon **pied** a glissé sur la dernière marche. J'ai tout de suite senti une douleur intense à la cheville. Après quelques **minutes**, j'ai pu me lever et appeler mon voisin. Il m'a aidé à marcher jusqu'à sa **voiture**. Les urgences de l'hôpital sont seulement à 5 **minutes** de chez moi. Je suis aux urgences depuis un peu plus d'une heure. J'ai attendu mon tour patiemment. Il n'y avait pas beaucoup de **monde** donc j'ai vu un docteur assez vite. L'infirmière m'a envoyé **faire** une radiographie pour vérifier que je n'avais pas de fracture. Heureusement, c'est seulement une entorse. Je vais **porter** une attelle pendant une semaine et utiliser des béquilles pour **marcher**. Plus de peur que de mal.

CHAPTER 42

1. **Un arc**
2. **Un arbre**
3. **Une carotte**
4. **Un carré**
5. **Une erreur**
6. **Le fer**
7. **Un jardin**
8. **Une larme**
9. **Lourd**
10. **Un miroir**
11. **Partager**
12. **Une porte**
13. **Un rideau**
14. **Rire**
15. **Un robinet**
16. **Un rond**
17. **Un sourire**
18. **Un travail**
19. **Trois**
20. **Un verre**

CHAPTER 43

Notre journée à Paris

7 – Une fois la visite de la tour Eiffel terminée, on se dirigera vers l'Arc de Triomphe.

10 – Une fois le déjeuner fini, on ira visiter le musée du Louvre.

3 – On a un million de choses à voir.

4 – On va commencer par la tour Eiffel.

14 – On a une longue journée devant nous !

6 – On a hâte !

13 – Ce soir, on a deux billets pour le Moulin Rouge.

1 – C'est la première fois qu'on visite Paris.

8 – Pour le déjeuner, on cherchera un restaurant près de l'Arc de Triomphe.

11 – Je veux voir la Joconde et les œuvres grecques.

5 – On a acheté des tickets en ligne pour aller tout en haut.

9 – Ça ne devrait pas être difficile à trouver.

12 – Je pense qu'on sera fatigués après le Louvre donc on ira sûrement boire un café avant de faire un tour en bateau mouche sur la Seine.

2 – On mange notre petit déjeuner avant d'attaquer la journée.

CHAPTER 44

1. Elle s'est cassé le **pied** gauche.
2. Est-ce que tu as **froid** ?
3. Regarde ce que tu as fait.
4. Le **crapaud** vient de sauter dans la marre.
5. Il fait **chaud** aujourd'hui !
6. Il est plus **grand** que je ne le pensais.
7. Appelle-moi **quand** tu arrives.
8. On a réservé la table ronde au restaurant.
9. Les oiseux travaillent dur pour construire leur **nid**.
10. Cette entreprise a été fondée il y a dix ans.
11. Qu'est-ce que tu **prends** pour dîner ?
12. Il y a toujours des **canards** dans ce parc.
13. Le **nord** est le contraire du sud.
14. On a trouvé un **accord**.
15. Elle a toujours été gourmande.
16. Il y a des travaux sur le **boulevard** aujourd'hui.
17. Il a un beau **regard**.
18. Je parle un petit peu **allemand**.
19. Il y a une araignée au **plafond**.
20. La loterie est un jeu de **hasard**.

CHAPTER 45

1. Trois – ~~Toi~~
2. Langue – ~~Longue~~
3. ~~Pain~~ – Paon
4. Je – ~~Jeu~~
5. ~~Rose~~ – Rase
6. Dos – ~~Doigt~~
7. ~~Chaud~~ – Chou
8. ~~Leur~~ – Lourd
9. Chaque – ~~Chacun~~
10. ~~Belle~~ – Balle
11. Tout – ~~Tôt~~
12. ~~Lent~~ – Long
13. Jeu – ~~Joue~~
14. Cheveux – ~~Chevaux~~
15. Paire – ~~Par~~
16. ~~Dessert~~ – Désert
17. Quatre – ~~Quart~~
18. Pâle – ~~Paille~~
19. ~~Pince~~ – Ponce
20. ~~Feuille~~ – Fouille

CHAPTER 46

Mon premier travail

J'ai décroché mon premier travail juste après l'université. J'ai passé **plusieurs entretiens**, et j'étais **très enthousiaste** à l'idée de commencer à travailler. Après **trois entretiens**, j'ai eu une offre d'emploi. Le premier jour, je **suis arrivé** à l'heure au bureau. Mes collègues **étaient accueillants** et m'ont montré les tâches à réaliser. L'ambiance **était agréable** et **les horaires** étaient parfaits pour moi. Après quelques semaines, j'avais déjà appris énormément et je me sentais de **plus en plus à** l'aise. Mon manager m'a vite donné de nouvelles responsabilités. J'ai travaillé **trois ans** dans cette entreprise avant de lancer mon propre business.

CHAPTER 47

1. Il **faut être patient dans** la **vie**.
2. Tu **penses** qu'**ils arriveront** à l'**heure** ?
3. On **boit toujours une tasse** de café **quand** on se **lève**.
4. Internet est **tellement lent** en ce **moment** !
5. Tu **peux** appeler ton **client avant** de partir ?
6. J'**étudie** l'**anglais** au **moins** une **heure** par jour.
7. Ce **meuble** est **plus grand** que je ne le **pensais**.
8. La **rentrée** des **classes** est en **septembre**.
9. Mon mari et moi **allons** voyager **après notre retraite**.
10. Le lac est **vide à cause** de la **sécheresse**.
11. J'ai lu ce **livre** en **deux jours**.
12. C'est bien d'**apprendre** du nouveau **vocabulaire tous** les **jours**.
13. Elle **veut** venir avec moi à la **piscine dimanche**.
14. Pourquoi est-ce que tu es **triste** ?
15. Je n'ai **aucune idée** de ce qu'elle **voulait dire** !
16. Tu **auras** ton cadeau le jour de ton **anniversaire**.
17. Je **pense** qu'**ils sont heureux ensemble**.
18. Il **faut** porter de la **crème solaire** pour protéger sa peau.
19. Les **vieilles personnes doivent** rester **actives** au quotidien.
20. **Elle** a mal **aux dents depuis** ce matin.

CHAPTER 48

1. ~~Bu~~ – Boue
2. Buche – ~~Bouche~~
3. Bulle – ~~Boule~~
4. ~~Du~~ – Doux
5. Jure – ~~Jour~~
6. ~~Jus~~ – Joue
7. Lu – ~~Loup~~
8. Nu – ~~Nous~~

9. ~~Pu~~ – Pou
10. Pull – ~~Poule~~
11. ~~Rue~~ – Roue
12. Russe – ~~Rousse~~

13. ~~Su~~ – Sous
14. ~~Sur~~ – Sourd
15. Tu – ~~Tout~~
16. Vue – ~~Vous~~

CHAPTER 49

Une soirée sans téléphone

10 – On essaye de ne pas parler de travail car on travaille ensemble.
4 – Au début, c'était un peu difficile mais maintenant, on laisse nos téléphones dans un tiroir et on n'y touche pas.
8 – C'est tellement bien de ne pas être interrompus par des notifications constantes.
3 – Cela nous permet d'être complétement présent, sans distractions.
1 – Chaque semaine, mon mari et moi essayons de passer une soirée ensemble.
5 – Pendant ces soirées, on fait des choses simples mais agréables.
7 – De temps en temps, on va au restaurant ou on va boire un verre.
11 – On attend toujours avec impatiente notre soirée car on se sent un peu coupés du monde.
6 – Parfois, on joue à des jeux de société, ou on cuisine ensemble un bon repas.
2 – Techniquement, on passe toutes nos soirées ensemble mais une fois par semaine, on passe une soirée sans téléphone.
9 – Cela nous permet de parler de nos projets et de la vie de tous les jours.

CHAPTER 50

Le jour on a planté un arbre

Le village où j'ai grandi se trouve au milieu d'une **forêt**. Cela ressemble à un paysage de carte postale. Il y a une **rivière** qui traverse le village. Il y a toujours des enfants qui s'y baignent quand il fait **chaud**. À chaque fois que je retourne au village, je me promène au bord de cette rivière. À la fin du sentier, il y a un **arbre** qu'on a planté quand j'étais à l'école. Je devais avoir 10 **ans** je pense. C'est un de mes meilleurs **souvenirs**. Cette année-là, on avait appris plein de choses sur les arbres et les **animaux**. Notre professeur nous avait montré comment reconnaître les différents arbres par leurs feuilles et les animaux par leurs empreintes. Je me souviens encore de mon **livre** avec les feuilles mortes collées sur chaque **page**. À la fin de l'année, notre classe a planté un arbre. C'était une vraie **aventure** à l'époque. Aujourd'hui, l'arbre a bien poussé. Il y a aussi une **plaque** avec le nom de notre classe et l'année où on l'a planté. C'est vraiment un **bon** souvenir.

FRENCH-ENGLISH GLOSSARY

A

À l'aise adv | *Comfortable*
À l'école | *At school*
À l'époque | *Back then*
À l'heure | *On time*
À l'intérieur adv | *Inside*
À la main adv | *By hand*
Une abeille nf | *A bee*
Abîmer v | *To damage*
Absent adj | *Absent*
Accéder v | *To access*
Un accent nm | *An accent*
Accepter v | *To accept*
Un accès nm | *An access*
Accessible adj | *Accessible*
Un accident nm | *An accident*
Accompagner v | *To accompany*
Un accord nm | *An agreement*
Accrocher v | *To hang*
Un accueil nm | *A welcome*
Accueillant – Accueillante adj | *Welcoming*
Accueillir v | *To welcome*
Un achat nm | *A purchase*
Acheter v | *To buy*
Actif – Active adj | *Active*
Une activité interactive nf + adj |
An interactive activity
Adapter v | *To adapt*
Admirer v | *To admire*
Adopter v | *To adopt*
Adorable adj | *Adorable*
Adorer v | *To like*
Un – Une adulte n | *An adult*
Un aéroport nm | *An airport*
Des affaires nf | *Stuffs*
Âgé – Âgée adj | *Older*
Agréable adj | *Pleasant*
De l'ail nm | *Garlic*

Aimer v | *To like*
Ajouter v | *To add*
Une alimentation nf | *A diet*
Allemand adj | *German*
Alors adv | *Then*
L'ambiance nf | *The atmosphere*
L'ambiance de Noël nf | *Christmas spirit*
Améliorer v | *To improve*
Amener v | *To bring*
Un ami – Une amie n | *A friend*
L'amour nf | *Love*
Une ampoule nf | *A lightbulb*
Des amuse-bouches nm | *Appetizers*
Une anecdote nf | *An anecdote*
L'anglais nm | *English*
Un animal – Des animaux nm |
An animal – Animals
Une année nf | *A year*
L'année dernière nf + adj | *Last year*
Un anniversaire nm | *A birthday*
Apercevoir v | *To see*
Un apéritif nm | *Aperitif*
Un appareil nm | *A device*
Un appartement nm | *An apartment*
Appeler v | *To call*
Apporter v | *To bring*
Apprendre v | *To learn*
Après adv | *After*
Un après-midi nm | *An afternoon*
Un aquarium nm | *An aquarium*
Une araignée nf | *A spider*
Un arbre nm | *A tree*
Un arc nm | *An arc*
L'Arc de Triomphe nm | *The Arc of Triomphe*
Une armoire nf | *A wardrobe*
Un arrêt de bus nm | *A bus stop*
Arrêter v | *To stop*
Arriver v | *To arrive*
Artificiel – Artificielle adj | *Artificial*

Un – Une artiste n | *An artist*
Athlétique adj | *Athletic*
Attaquer v | *To start*
Atteindre v | *To reach*
Une attelle nf | *A splint*
Attendre avec impatiente | *To look forward to*
Attendre v | *To wait*
Au loin adv | *In the distance*
Au milieu de adv | *In the middle of*
Au moins adv | *At least*
Au total adv | *In total*
L'automne nm | *Fall*
Une autoroute nf | *A highway*
Les autres nm | *The others*
Avant adv | *Before*
Un avis nm | *An opinion*
Un avocat nm | *An avocado*
Avoir … ans v | *To be … years*
Avoir faim v | *To be hungry*
Avoir froid v | *To be cold*
Avoir hâte v | *Can't wait*
Avoir honte v | *To be ashamed*
Avoir l'impression v | *To feel like*
Avoir mal v | *To be in pain*
Avril nm | *April*

B

Une bague nf | *A ring*
Un bail nm | *A lease*
Un bain nm | *A bath*
Baisser v | *To lower*
Une balade nf | *A walk*
Une balance nf | *A scale*
Une balle nf | *A ball*
Une banane nf | *A banana*
Un banc nm | *A bench*
Une banderole nf | *A banner*
Une banque nf | *A bank*
Une barre nf | *A bar*
Une barre protéinée nf | *A protein bar*
Un bas nm | *A stocking*

Une bataille nf | *A battle*
Un bateau mouche nm | *A riverboat*
Une batterie portable nf | *A large battery*
Un bâtiment nm | *A building*
De la batterie nf | *Battery*
Beau – Belle adj | *Beautiful*
Une belle journée adj + nf | *A beautiful day*
Des béquilles nf | *Crutches*
Bête adj | *Stupid*
Du beurre nm | *Butter*
Du beurre de cacao nm | *Cocoa butter*
Bien payé – payée adv + adj | *Well paid*
Bientôt adv | *Soon*
Des bijoux nm | *Jewels*
Une bille nf | *A ball*
Un billet nm | *A ticket*
Une bise nf | *A kiss*
Bizarre adj | *Weird*
Une blague nf | *A joke*
Blanc – Blanche adj | *White*
Du blé nm | *Wheat*
Boire un café | *To drink a coffee*
Boire un verre | *To have a drink*
Boire v | *To drink*
Les bois nm | *The woods*
Une boisson nf | *A drink*
Une boîte nf | *A box*
Une boîte de conserve nf | *A can*
Un bol de glace nm | *A bowl of ice cream*
Un bon nm | *A voucher*
Bon – Bonne adj | *Good*
Un bon livre adj + nm | *A good book*
Un bon repas adj + nm | *A good meal*
Un bonbon nm | *A candy*
Un bond nm | *A jump*
La bouche nf | *The mouth*
De la boue nf | *Mud*
Bouger v | *To move*
Une bougie nf | *A candle*
Une boule nf | *A ball*
Bouillir v | *To boil*
Une bouilloire nf | *A kettle*
Du bouillon nm | *Broth*

Le boulanger nm | *The baker*
Une boulangerie nf | *A bakery*
Un boulevard nm | *A boulevard*
Une bouteille nf | *A bottle*
Une bouteille d'eau nf | *A water bottle*
Une bouteille de champagne nf |
A bottle of champagne
Un bras nm | *An arm*
Briller v | *To shine*
Une brise nf | *A breeze*
Du brouillard nm | *Fog*
Un brouillon nm | *A draft*
Le bruit nm | *Noise*
Brun – Brune adj | *Brown*
Bu (Boire) v | *Drank (To drink)*
Une buche nf | *A log*
Un budget nm | *A budget*
Une bulle nf | *A bubble*
Un bureau nm | *A desk*
Un bureau nm | *An office*
Un bus nm | *A bus*
Un business nm | *A business*
Un but nm | *A goal*

C

C'est dommage | *That's too bad*
Une cabane nf | *A shed*
Une cabine nf | *A changing room*
Cacher v | *To hide*
Un caddie nm | *A shopping cart*
Un cadeau nm | *A gift*
Un cadre nm | *A frame*
Un café nm | *A cafe*
Un café nm | *A coffee*
Du café moulu nm + adj | *Ground coffee*
Une cage nf | *A cage*
Un caillou nm | *A rock*
Un caissier – Une caissière n | *A cashier*
Calme adj | *Calm*
Calmement adv | *Calmly*
Camille nf | *Camille*

Un camion nm | *A truck*
La camomille nf | *Chamomille*
Le camping nm | *Camping*
Un camping-car nm | *A motorhome*
Un canard nm | *A duck*
Un canon nm | *A cannon*
Une carotte nf | *A carrot*
Un carré nm | *A square*
Une carte nf | *A map*
Une carte bancaire nf | *A bank card*
Une carte postale nf | *A postcard*
Un casier nm | *A locker*
Casser v | *To break*
Ce soir nf | *Tonight*
Célibataire adj | *Single*
Un cercueil nm | *A coffin*
Un cerf nm | *A deer*
Ces adj | *These*
Cette année nf | *This year*
Chacun – Chacune pr | Each
Chacun adj | *Each*
Une chaise de jardin nf | *A garden chair*
Une chambre nf | *A bedroom*
Un champion nm | *A champion*
Une chance nf | *A chance*
Un chandail nm | *A sweater*
Changer v | *To change*
Chanter v | *To sing*
Un chapeau nm | *A hat*
Chaque adj | *Each*
Charger v | *To charge*
Un chargeur nm | *A charger*
La chasse nf | *Hunt*
Chasser v | *To hunt*
Un chat nm | *A cat*
Un château gonflable nm | *A bouncy castle*
Un château nm | *A castle*
Chaud – Chaude adj | *Hot*
Chaud adj | *Hot*
Des chaussures de marche nf | *Walking shoes*
Le chemin du retour nm | *The way back*
Une chenille nf | *A caterpillar*
Cher – Chère adj | *Expensive*

Chercher v | *To get – To pick up*
Chercher v | *To look for*
Un cheval – Des chevaux nm |
A horse – Horses
Des chevaux nm | *Horses*
Des cheveux nm | *Hair*
Une cheville nf | *An ankle*
Un chevreuil nm | *A deer*
Chiant – Chiante adj | *Annoying*
Un chien nm | *A dog*
Des chips nf | *Chips*
Du chocolat blanc nm | *White chocolate*
Du chocolat chaud nm | *Hot chocolate*
Choisir v | *To choose*
Un choix nm | *A choice*
Une chose nf | *A thing*
Une chose à voir | *A thing to see*
Un chou nm | *A cabbage*
Chouette adj | *Nice*
Une chouette façon nf + adj | *A nice way*
Le ciel nm | *The sky*
Un cinéma nm | *A cinema*
Un cintre nm | *A hanger*
Une citrouille nf | *A pumpkin*
Une classe nf | *A class*
Une clé nf | *A key*
Un client – Une cliente n | *A customer*
Un cochon nm | *A pig*
Un colis nm | *A package*
Collé – Collée pp | *Stuck*
Un – Une collègue n | *A colleague*
Coller v | *To glue*
Un combat nm | *A fight*
Commander v | *To order*
Commencer v | *To begin*
Complet – Complète adj | *Complete*
Compliqué – Compliquée adj | *Complicated*
Compter v | *To plan*
Un compteur nm | *An odometer*
Conduire v | *To drive*
De la confiture nf | *Jam*
Confortable adj | *Comfortable*
Un congélateur nm | *A freezer*

Un conseil nm | *An advice*
Conseiller v | *To advise*
Constant – Constante adj | *Constant*
Construire v | *To build*
Content – Contente adj | *Happy*
Le contraire nm | *The opposite*
Un contrat nm | *A contract*
Un copain nm | *A friend*
Une coquille nf | *A shell*
Une corbeille nf | *A trash can*
Une corneille nf | *A crow*
Un corps nm | *A body*
Le cou nm | *The neck*
Coule (Couler) v | *To flow*
Une couleur nf | *A color*
Une couleur vive nf + adj | *A bright color*
Une coupure de courant nf | *A power outage*
Courir v | *To run*
Une course nf | *A race*
Court – Courte adj | *Short*
Un coussin nm | *A cushion*
Coûter v | *To cost*
Craindre v | *To fear*
Un crapaud nm | *A toad*
De la crème nf | *Cream*
De la crème pour les mains nf | *Hand cream*
La crème solaire nf | *Sunscreen*
Croire v | *To believe*
Une croix nf | *A cross*
Une cruche nf | *A pot*
Cueillir v | *To pick*
Une cuillère nf | *A spoon*
Une cuisine nf | *A kitchen*
Cuisiner v | *To cook*
Cuire v | *To bake*
La culture nf | *Culture*

D

... de nos rêves | *... of our dream*
Dans prep | *In*
Une danse nf | *A dance*

Décembre nm | *December*
Décharger v | *To unload*
Décider v | *To decide*
De la décoration nf | *Decorations*
Découvrir v | *To discover*
Décrocher v | *To land*
Dedans adv | *Inside*
Déguster v | *To enjoy*
Un déjeuner nm | *A lunch*
Délicieux adj | *Delicious*
Demander v | *To ask*
Démolir v | *To demolish*
Une déneigeuse nf | *A snow plow*
Une dent nf | *A tooth*
Un dentiste nm | *A dentist*
Le dernier voyage adj + nm | *The last trip*
Derrière adv | *Behind*
Des art | *Some*
Descendre v | *To go down*
Un désert nm | *A desert*
Du désinfectant nm | *Hand sanitizer*
Un dessert nm | *A dessert*
Un dessin nm | *A drawing*
Dessous adv | *Below*
Dessus adv | *Above*
Un détail nm | *A detail*
Détester v | *To hate*
Détruire v | *To tear down*
Le deuil nm | *Mourning*
Deux n | *Two*
La deuxième nf | *The second*
Devant adv | *In front of*
Devenir v | *To become*
Un diamant nm | *A diamond*
Différent – Différente adj | *Different*
Difficile adj | *Difficult*
Le dimanche nm | *Sunday*
Un dîner nm | *A dinner*
Dire v | *To say*
Une direction nf | *A direction*
Disparaître v | *To disappear*
Une distraction nf | *A distraction*
Une dizaine de minutes | *About ten minutes*

Un documentaire nm | *A documentary*
Des documents d'identités nm |
Identity documents/ID
Un docteur nm | *A doctor*
Un doigt nm | *A finger*
Dommage adj | *Too bad*
Donner v | *To give*
Dormir v | *To sleep*
Le dos nm | *Back*
Douillet – Douillette adj | *Cozy*
Une douleur intense nf + adj | *An intense pain*
Doux – Douce adj | *Soft*
Un dragon nm | *A dragon*
Un drap de lit nm | *A bed sheet*
Du art | *Some*
Dur – Dure adj | *Hard*
Durer v | *To last*

E

De l'eau nf | *Water*
Les eaux usées nf | *Wastewater*
Une écharpe nf | *A scarf*
Une école nf | *A school*
Écrire v | *To text*
Un écureuil nm | *A squirrel*
Égoïste adj | *Selfish*
Une élection nf | *An election*
Un éléphant nm | *An elephant*
Elle entend (Entendre) v |
She listens (To listen)
Elle lit (Lire) v | *She is reading (To read)*
Elle marche (Marcher) v |
She is walking (To walk)
Elle pr | *She*
Elle se détend (Se détendre) v |
She is relaxing (To relax)
Elle tient (Tenir) v | *She is holding (To hold)*
Elles chantent (Chanter) v |
They are singing (To sing)
Elles parlent (Parler) v |
They are speaking (To speak)

Elles pr | *They*

Emballer v | *To wrap*

Embêtant – Embêtante adj | *Annoying*

Emmener v | *To take away*

Empilé – Empilée adj | *Stacked*

Un employé nm | *An employee*

Emporter v | *To take away*

Une empreinte nf | *A footprint*

En arrière adv | *Back*

En automne | *In the fall*

En ce moment | *Right now*

En ligne adv | *Online*

En mauvais état adj | *In a bad shape*

En plein air adv | *Open-air*

En retard adv | *Late*

En revanche | *On the other hand*

En valoir la peine | *To be worth it*

Enchanté – Enchantée adj | *Delighted*

Un enclos nm | *An enclosure*

Encourager v | *To cheer*

De l'endurance nf | *Endurance*

Un – Une enfant n | *A child*

Énorme adj | *Huge*

Ensemble adv | *Together*

Entendre v | *To hear*

Enthousiaste adj | *Excited*

Une entorse nf | *A sprain*

Une entreprise nf | *A company*

Un entretien nm | *An interview*

Des épices nf | *Spices*

Un épouvantail nm | *A scarecrow*

Un époux nm | *A spouse*

Un escargot nm | *A snail*

L'essentiel nm | *The essential*

Une erreur nf | *A mistake*

Un étang nm | *A pond*

L'été nm | *Summer*

Éteindre v | *To turn off*

Être abîmé – abîmée v | *To be damaged*

Être démoli(e) v | *To be demolished*

Être en panne v | *To be out of order*

Être fermé – fermée v | *To be closed*

Être gêné – gênée v | *To be embarassed*

Être habitué – habituée v | *To be used to*

Être interrompu – interrompue v |
To be interrupted

Être limité – limitée v | *To be limited*

Être motivé – motivée v | *To be motivated*

Être préparé – préparée v | *To be prepared*

Être présent – présente v | *To be present*

Être tombé – tombée v | *To fall*

Étudier v | *To study*

Un euro nm | *A euro*

Un éventail nm | *A fan*

Exister v | *To exist*

Un exploit sportif nm | *A sporting achievement*

F

Fabriquer v | *To make*

Une façon nf | *A way*

Une facture nf | *A bill*

Faire v | *To do*

Faire attention v | *Be careful – Watch out*

Faire beau v | *To be nice*

Faire chaud v | *To be hot*

Faire du camping | *To camp*

Faire du sport nm | *To exercise*

Faire froid v | *To be cold*

Faire le plein v | *To fill up*

Faire les courses | *To shop*

Faire mal v | *To hurt*

Faire mauvais v | *To be bad (weather)*

Faire peur v | *To scare*

Faire un tour | *To take a ride*

Une famille nf | *A family*

La famille nf | *Family*

Un fantôme nm | *A ghost*

De la farine nf | *Flour*

Un fauteuil nm | *An armchair*

Faux – Fausse adj | *False*

Un fermier nm | *A farmer*

Une fenêtre nf | *A window*

Le fenouil nm | *Fennel*

Le fer nm | *Iron*

Une fête d'anniversaire nf | *A birthday party*
Fêter v | *To celebrate*
Un feu nm | *A city light*
Un feu nm | *A fire*
Un feu ouvert nm | *An open fire*
Une feuille nf | *A leaf*
Une feuille morte nf + adj | *A dead leaf*
Février nm | *February*
Une file nf | *A line*
Une fille nf | *A daughter*
Un film nm | *A film*
Un fils nm | *A son*
La fin nf | *The end*
La fin du mois nf | *The end of the month*
La fin du monde nf | *The end of the world*
Finir v | *To finish*
Une fleur nf | *A flower*
Des fleurs nf | *Flowers*
Flexible adj | *Flexible*
Une fois nf | *Once*
Fonctionner v | *To work*
Fonder v | *To found*
Une forêt nf | *A forest*
Fou – Folle adj | *Crazy*
Une fouille nf | *A search*
Fouiller v | *To rummage*
Un foulard nm | *A scarf*
Une fourmi nf | *An ant*
Une fracture nf | *A fracture*
Frais – Fraîche adj | *Cool*
Une fraise nf | *A strawberry*
Une framboise nf | *A raspberry*
Un Français – Une Française n |
A French person
Le français nm | *French*
La France nf | *France*
Franchir v | *To cross*
Un frein nm | *A brake*
Un frigo nm | *A fridge*
Froid adj | *Cold*
Des fruits nm | *Fruits*
Le futur nm | *Future*

G

Un gagnant nm | *A winner*
Gagner v | *To win*
Gai – Gaie adj | *Pleasant*
Galant adj | *Gallant*
Un garage nm | *A garage*
Un – Une garde n | *A guard*
Garder v | *To keep*
Une gare nf | *A train station*
Une gargouille nf | *A gargoyle*
Gargouiller v | *To gurgle*
Gaspiller v | *To waste*
Un gâteau nm | *A cake*
Gauche adj | *Left*
Gazouiller v | *To babble*
Un générateur nm | *A generator*
Généreux – Généreuse adj | *Generous*
Des genoux nm | *Knees*
Les gens nm | *People*
Gentille adj | *Kind*
De la glace nf | *Ice cream*
Glisser v | *To slip*
Une gourde nf | *A gourd*
Une gorgée nf | *A sip*
Gourmand adj | *Greedy*
Le goût nm | *Taste*
Goûter v | *To taste*
Une goutte nf | *A drop*
Un grain nm | *A grain*
Grand – Grande adj | *Big*
Le grand jour nm | *The big day*
Grandir v | *To grow up*
Gras – Grasse adj | *Fat – Oily*
Grave adj | *Serious*
Une grenouille nf | *A frog*
Gribouiller v | *To scribble*
Grignoter v | *To snack*
Une grille nf | *A grid*
Griller v | *To grill*
Gris – Grise adj | *Gray*
Gros – Grosse adj | *Big*

Un gros mammifère adj + nm | *A big mammal*
Un gros projet adj + nm | *A big project*
Un groupe nm | *A group*
Une groseille nf | *A gooseberry*
Une guerre nf | *A war*
Un – Une guide n | *A guide*

H

Un habit nm | *A piece of clothing*
Un habitant – Une habitante n | *A resident*
Habiter v | *To live*
Une habitude nf | *A habit*
Des habits nm | *Clothes*
Le hasard nm | *Chance*
L'herbe nf | *Grass*
Une heure nf | *An hour*
L'heure d'ouverture nf | *Opening time*
Heureux – Heureuse adj | *Happy*
Des hiboux nm | *Owls*
Hier adv | *Yesterday*
L'hiver nm | *Winter*
Un homme nm | *A man*
Un hôpital nm | *A hospital*
Les horaires nm | *Hours*
Un hôtel nm | *A hotel*
Humble adj | *Humble*

I

Il pr | *He*
Il chante (Chanter) v | *He is singing (To sing)*
Il comprend (Comprendre) v |
He understands (To understand)
Il dit (Dire) v | *He is saying (To say)*
Il prend (Prendre) v | *He takes (To take)*
Il vient (Venir) v | *He comes (To come)*
Ils dorment (Dormir) v |
They are sleeping (To sleep)
Ils mangent (Manger) v |
They are eating (To eat)

Ils pr | *They*
Immense adj | *Huge*
Un immeuble nm | *A building*
Impatiemment adv | *Impatiently*
Impossible adj | *Impossible*
Inclure v | *To include*
Incroyable adj | *Incredible*
Une idée nf | *An idea*
Un incident nm | *An incident*
Une infirmière nf | *A nurse*
Une information nf | *Information*
Un ingrédient nm | *An ingredient*
Inquiet adj | *Worried*
Installer v | *To set up*
Un instant nm | *A moment*
Intéressant – Intéressante adj | *Interesting*
Interminable adj | *Endless*
Internet nm | *Internet*
Italien adj | *Italian*

J

Jaloux – Jalouse adj | *Jealous*
Jamais adv | *Never*
Une jambe nf | *A leg*
Un jambon nm | *Ham*
Un jardin nm | *A garden*
Un jardinier nm | *A gardener*
Jaune adj | *Yellow*
Je pr | *I*
Je comprends (Comprendre) v |
I understand (To understand)
Je dis (Dire) v | *I say (To say)*
Je finis (Finir) v | *I finish (To finish)*
Je garde (Garder) v | *I am keeping (To keep)*
Je parle (Parler) v | *I am speaking (To speak)*
Je peux (Pouvoir) v | *I can (To be able to)*
Un jeu nm | *A game*
Un jeu de société nm | *A board game*
Jeune adj | *Young*
Les Jeux Olympiques nm | *The Olympic Games*
La Joconde nf | *The Mona Lisa*

Une jonquille nf | *A dafodill*
Une joue nf | *A cheek*
Joli – Jolie adj | *Pretty*
Jouer v | *To play*
Un jouet nm | *A toy*
Un jour nm | *A day*
Une journée nf | *A day*
Une journée de congé nf | *A day off*
Juillet nm | *July*
Jurer v | *To swear*
Du jus nm | *Juice*

K

Un kilomètre nm | *A kilometre*
km/h – kilomètre heure |
km/h – kilometre hour

L

Un lac nm | *A lake*
Laisser v | *To give*
Le lait d'amandes nm | *Almond milk*
Le lait de soja nm | *Soy milk*
Une larme nf | *A tear*
Une lampe nf | *A lamp*
Une langue nf | *A language*
Large adj | *Big*
Une lasagne nf | *A lasagna*
Laver v | *To wash*
La lecture nf | *Reading*
Des légumes nm | *Vegetables*
Lent – Lente adj | *Slow*
Lentement adv | *Slowly*
Une lentille nf | *A lens*
Les art | *The*
Une lettre nf | *A letter*
Leur pr | *Their*
Levé – Levée pp | *Risen*
Lever v | *To lift*
De la levure nf | *Yeast*

Libre adj | *Free*
Un lieu nm | *A place*
La ligne d'arrivée nf | *The finish line*
Lire v | *To read*
Une liste de courses nf | *A shopping list*
Un lit nm | *A bed*
Un livre nm | *A book*
Livrer v | *To deliver*
Lointain adj | *Distant*
Londres | *London*
Long – Longue adj | *Long*
Une longue balade adj + nm | *A long walk*
La loterie nf | *The lottery*
Louer v | *To rent*
Un loup nm | *A wolf*
Lourd – Lourde adj | *Heavy*
Lu (Lire) v | *Read (To read)*
Le lundi nm | *Monday*
Des lunettes nf | *Glasses*

M

Une machine nf | *A machine*
Une machine à laver nf | *A washing machine*
Une machine à pain nf | *A bread machine*
Un magasin nm | *A store*
Un magasin de sport nm | *A sport shop*
Une maille nf | *A stitch*
Un maillot nm | *A swimsuit*
Une main nf | *A hand*
Maintenant adv | *Now*
La maire nf | *The mayor*
Une maison nf | *A house*
Malade adj | *Sick*
Maman nf | *Mom*
Un manager nm | *A manager*
Manger v | *To eat*
Un manteau nm | *A coat*
Un marathon nm | *A marathon*
Une marche nf | *A step*
Une marche nf | *A walk*
Un marché nm | *A market*

Un marché de Noël nm | *A Christmas Market*
Marcher v | *To walk*
Un mari nm | *A husband*
Un mariage nm | *A wedding*
Une marre nf | *A pond*
Marseille nf | *Marseille*
Un matelas gonflable nm |
An inflatable mattress
Un matin nm | *A morning*
Le matin nm | *Morning*
Me pr | *Me*
Une médaille nf | *A medal*
Une médaille d'or nf | *A gold medal*
Meilleur – Meilleure adj | *Best*
La meilleure façon adj + nf | *The best way*
La meilleure place adj + nf | *The best place*
Un meilleur souvenir adj + nm | *A best memory*
Mélanger v | *To mix*
La mémoire nf | *The memory*
Le ménage nm | *Cleaning*
Un menton nm | *A chin*
La mer nf | *The sea*
Une mère nf | *A mother*
Merveilleux – Merveilleuse adj | *Wonderful*
Mes adj | *My*
Du métal nm | *Metal*
La météo nf | *The weather*
Un mètre nm | *A metre*
Mettre v | *To add*
Mettre au four v | *To put in the oven*
Mettre la table v | *To set the table*
Un meuble nm | *A piece of furniture*
Un millefeuille nm | *A mille-feuille (pastry)*
Un million nm | *A million*
Minuscule adj | *Tiny*
Un miroir nm | *A mirror*
Moi pr | *Me*
Un moine nm | *A monk*
Moins adv | *Less*
Un mois nm | *A month*
Le monde nm | *The world*
Un monstre nm | *A monster*

Une montagne nf | *A mountain*
Une montre nf | *A watch*
Montrer v | *To show*
Une mouche nf | *A fly*
La mousse nf | *The foam*
Un mur nm | *A wall*
Murmurer v | *To whisper*
Un musée nm | *A museum*
Le musée du Louvre nm | *The Louvre Museum*
Une musique de Noël nf | *Christmas music*

N

Nager v | *To swim*
Une narine nf | *A nostril*
La nature nf | *Nature*
Ne ... jamais | *Never*
Ne ... pas | *Not*
Ne ... plus | *No more*
Nécessaire adj | *Necessary*
Neiger v | *To snow*
Nerveux – Nerveuse adj | *Nervous*
Nettoyer v | *To clean*
Un nid nm | *A nest*
Noël nm | *Christmas*
Noir – Noire adj | *Black*
Une noix nf | *A nut*
Un nom nm | *A name*
Le nord nm | *The North*
Nostalgique adj | *Nostalgic*
Une notification nf | *A notification*
Une note nf | *A note*
Notre pr | *Our*
Des nouilles nf | *Noodles*
Nourrir v | *To feed*
De la nourriture nf | *Food*
Nous dansons (Danser) v |
We are dancing (To dance)
Nous faisons (Faire) v | *We are doing (To do)*
Nous pr | *We*
Nous voyons (Voir) v | *We see (To see)*

Nouveau – Nouvelle adj | *New*
Novembre nm | *November*
Nu – Nue adj | *Naked*
La nuit nf | *The night*
La nuit dernière nf + adj | *Last night*
Nulle part adv | *Nowhere*

O

Un objectif nm | *A goal*
Un objet nm | *An object*
Observer v | *To watch*
Occupé – Occupée adj | *Busy*
Une odeur nf | *A smell*
Un œil nm | *An eye*
Des œufs nm | *Eggs*
Une œuvre grecque nf + adj | *A Greek work*
Une offre d'emploi nf | *A job offer*
Un oiseau nm | *A bird*
On pr | *We*
On attend (Attendre) v |
We are waiting (To wait)
On devient (Devenir) v |
We become (To become)
On discute (Discuter) v |
We are talking (To talk)
On interdit (Interdire) v |
We forgive (To forgive)
On regarde (Regarder) v |
We are watching (To watch)
On reprend (Reprendre) v |
We are restarting (To restart)
Un oncle nm | *An uncle*
Une opinion nf | *An opinion*
Une option nf | *An option*
Une orange nf | *An orange*
Un ordinateur nm | *A computer*
Un ordinateur portable nm | *A laptop*
L'orgueil nm | *Pride*
Une oreille nf | *An ear*
Un oreiller nm | *A pillow*

Organiser v | *To organize*
Un orteil nm | *A toe*
Oublier v | *To forget*
Un ours nm | *A bear*
Un outil nm | *A tool*
Ouvrir v | *To open*
Ouvrir ses portes | *To open its doors*

P

Une page nf | *A page*
Un paillasson nm | *A doormat*
Une paille nf | *A straw*
De la paille nf | *Straw*
Un pain nm | *A loaf of bread*
Du pain nm | *Bread*
Du pain à l'ail nm | *Garlic bread*
Un pain d'épices nm | *A gingerbread*
Une paire nf | *A pair*
La paix nf | *Peace*
Pâle adj | *Pale*
Un panier de linge nm | *A basket of laundry*
Un pantalon nm | *A pair of pants*
Un paon nm | *A peacock*
Un papillon nm | *A butterfly*
Un paquet de mouchoirs nm | *A pack of tissues*
Par prep | *By*
Un parc nm | *A park*
Pardon | *Pardon*
Pareil – Pareille adj | *Same*
Un parent nm | *A parent*
Les parents nm | *Parents*
Parfait – Parfaite adj | *Perfect*
Parfait adj | *Perfect*
Parler v | *To speak*
Parler v | *To talk*
Partager v | *To share*
Partir v | *To leave*
Partir à la retraite | *To retire*
Partout adv | *Eveywhere*
Un pas nm | *A step*

Pas de problème | *No problem*

Un passage nm | *A visit*

Un passage secret nm + adj | *A secret passage*

Un passeport nm | *A passport*

Passer v | *To come (for transportation)*

Passer v | *To have*

Passer v | *To pass*

Passer des heures | *To spend hours*

Passer du temps | *To spend time*

La pâte nf | *The dough*

Des pâtes nf | *Pasta*

Patient – Patiente adj | *Patient*

Un patron nm | *A boss*

Une patrouille nf | *A patrol*

Pauvre adj | *Poor*

Payer v | *To pay*

Un pays nm | *A country*

Un paysage nm | *A landscape*

La peau nf | *Skin*

Peindre v | *To paint*

Un peintre nm | *A painter*

Une pelle à neige nf | *A snow shovel*

Pendre v | *To hung*

Penser v | *To think*

Perdre v | *To lose*

Perdre son temps v | *To waste time*

Le père nm | *The father*

Permettre v | *To allow*

Une personne nf | *A person*

Personne pr | *Nobody*

Petit – Petite adj | *Little*

Un petit appartement adj + nm |
A small apartment

Un petit cahier adj + nm | *A small notebook*

Un petit déjeuner nm | *A breakfast*

Un petit groupe adj + nm | *A little group*

Un petit village adj + nm | *A little village*

Une petite bouteille adj + nf | *A little bottle*

Les petites annonces nf | *The classified ads*

Pétrir v | *To knead*

Les petits et les grands | *Young and old*

Un peu adj | *A little*

Une peur nf | *A fear*

Une pièce nf | *A room*

Un peu adj | *A little*

Un pied nm | *A foot*

Un pigeon nm | *A pigeon*

Une pile nf | *A pile*

Une pince nf | *A pliers*

Une piscine nf | *A swimming pool*

Des pizzas nf | *Pizzas*

Un placard nm | *A cupboard*

Une place nf | *Room*

Le plafond nm | *The ceiling*

Une plage nf | *A beach*

Un plan nm | *A plan*

Un plan de travail nm | *A countertop*

Une planche nf | *A board*

Une plante nf | *A plant*

Planter v | *To plant*

Une plaque nf | *A plaque*

Un plat nm | *A dish*

Un plateau nm | *A tray*

Plein – Pleine adj | *Full*

Pleuvoir v | *To rain*

Une plume nf | *A feather*

Du poison nm | *Poison*

Un poisson nm | *A fish*

Du poivre nm | *Pepper*

Un pôle nm | *A pole*

Un pont nm | *A bridge*

Un port nm | *A port*

Un portail nm | *An entrance*

Une porte nf | *A door*

Un portefeuille nm | *A wallet*

Une potion nf | *A potion*

Un pou nm | *A louse*

Une poule nf | *A chicken*

Un poussin nm | *A chick*

La pompe à essence nf | *The gas station*

Ponce (Poncer) v | *To sand*

Porter v | *To carry*

Poser des problèmes | *To cause problems*

Pour prep | *For*

Des pours et des contres | *Pros and cons*
Pousser v | *To grow*
Le pouvoir nm | *Power*
Préférer v | *To prefer*
Premier – Première adj | *First*
La première | *The first*
La première fois adj + nf | *A first day*
La première fois adj + nf | *The first time*
Prendre v | *To have (drinks)*
Prendre v | *To take*
Prendre sa retraite | *To retire*
Prendre son bus v | *To catch a bus*
Prendre un café | *To have a coffee*
Préparer v | *To make*
Le présent nm | *The present*
Présent – Présente adj | *Present*
Préserver v | *To preserve*
Prêt – Prête adj | *Ready*
Prévoir v | *To call for*
Le printemps nm | *Spring*
Une prison nf | *A prison*
Un prix nm | *A price*
Un problème nm | *A problem*
Prochain – Prochaine adj | *Next*
Productif – Productive adj | *Productive*
Un produit nm | *A product*
Un produit artisanal nm + adj | *Craft*
Un produit de beauté nm | *A beauty product*
Un professeur nm | *A professor*
Un projet nm | *A project*
Une promenade nf | *A walk*
Propre adj | *Clean*
Propre adj | *Own*
Un – Une propriétaire n | *The owners*
Protéger v | *To protect*
Des protéines nf | *Proteins*
Une province nf | *A province*
Le public nm | *The public*
Un pull nm | *A sweater*
Pur – Pure adj | *Pure*

Q

Quand adv | *When*
Un quart nm | *A quarter*
Un quartier nm | *A neighborhood*
Quatre | *Four*
Quelque chose pr | *Something*
Une question nf | *A question*
Une quille nf | *A bowling pin*
Quitter v | *To leave*
Quotidien – Quotidienne adj | *Daily*

R

Un raccourci nm | *A shortcut*
Une radiographie nf | *An x-ray*
La rage nf | *Rabies*
Le rail nm | *Rail*
Ramasser v | *To collect*
Une randonnée nf | *A hike*
Du rangement nm | *Tidying*
Ranger v | *To tidy up*
Un rapport nm | *A report*
Rare adj | *Rare*
Rase (Raser) v | *To shave*
Rassurer v | *To reassure*
Une ratatouille nf | *A ratatouille*
Ravi – Ravie adj | *Delighted*
Réaliser v | *To carry out*
Récent – Récente adj | *Recent*
Recevoir v | *To get*
Réchauffer v | *To warm up*
Reconnaître v | *To recognize*
Reculer v | *To back*
Le regard nm | *A look*
Regarder v | *To look*
Une région nf | *A region*
Relier v | *To connect*
Rempli – Remplie adj | *Busy*
Remplir v | *To fill*
La Renaissance nf | *The Renaissance*

Un rendez-vous nm | *An appointment*
Une rénovation nf | *A renovation*
La rentrée des classes nf | *Start of school*
Rentrer v | *To return*
Renverser v | *To knock over*
Renvoyer v | *To send back*
Réparer v | *To repair*
Un repas nm | *A meal*
Un repas simple nm + adj | *A simple meal*
Reposer v | *To rest*
Un reptile nm | *A reptile*
Réserver v | *To book*
Résonner v | *To echo*
Résoudre v | *To resolve*
Une responsabilité nf | *A responsibility*
Responsable adj | *Responsible*
Ressembler v | *To look like*
Un restaurant nm | *A restaurant*
Le reste nm | *The rest*
Rester v | *To stay*
Le résultat nm | *The result*
La retraite nf | *Retirement*
Retourner v | *To go back*
Une réunion nf | *A meeting*
Réunir v | *To reunite*
Un rêve nm | *A dream*
Un réveil nm | *An alarm clock*
Un rideau nm | *A curtain*
Rire v | *To laugh*
Une rive nf | *A shore*
Une rivière nf | *A river*
Un robinet nm | *A faucet*
Un romain nm | *A Roman*
Un roman nm | *A novel*
Rond adj | *Round*
Un rond nm | *A round*
Rose adj | *Pink*
Une roue nf | *A wheel*
Rouge adj | *Red*
Rouiller v | *To rust*
Roule (Rouler) v | *To roll*
La route nf | *The road*

Roux – Rousse adj | *Redhead*
Une rue nf | *A street*
Une rupture nf | *A break up*
Russe adj | *Russian*

S

S'appeler v | *To be called*
S'arrêter v | *To stop*
S'entraîner v | *To practice*
S'habiller v | *To get dressed*
S'imprégner v | *To soak up*
S'installer v | *To settle in*
Un sac nm | *A bag*
Un sac nm | *A purse*
Un sac réutilisable nm + adj | *A reusable bag*
Une saison nf | *A season*
Sale adj | *Dirty*
Salissant – Salissante adj | *Messy*
Un salon nm | *A living room*
Un salon de coiffure nm | *A hair salon*
Samedi nm | *Saturday*
Sans adv | *Without*
Un sapin nm | *A pine tree*
Un sapin géant nm + adj | *A giant tree*
Sauter v | *To jump*
Une saveur nf | *A flavor*
Savoir v | *To know*
Se baigner v | *To swim*
Se brosser les dents v | *To brush your teeth*
Se casser v | *To break*
Se changer v | *To change*
Se concentrer v | *To focus*
Se débrouiller v | *To get by*
Se dépêcher v | *To hurry*
Se dérouler v | *To take place*
Se diriger v | *To head*
Se doucher v | *To shower*
Se faire mal v | *To hurt yourself*
Se fouler v | *To sprain*
Se lever v | *To get up*

Se maquiller v | *To put on makeup*
Se poser v | *To land*
Se préparer v | *To get ready*
Se promener v | *To walk*
Se rejoindre v | *To meet*
Se reposer v | *To rest*
Se réunir v | *To come together*
Se réveiller v | *To wake up*
Se sentir coupé v | *To feel cut off*
Se sentir v | *To feel*
Se servir v | *To use*
Se souvenir v | *To remember*
Se trouver v | *To be (located)*
Un sèche-linge nm | *A dryer*
La sécheresse nf | *Drought*
Un séjour nm | *A stay*
Du sel nm | *Salt*
Une semaine nf | *A week*
Sembler v | *To seem*
Un sentier nm | *A trail*
Sentir v | *To feel*
Sentir v | *To smell*
Septembre nm | *September*
Sérieux – Sérieuse adj | *Serious*
Un serpent nm | *A snake*
Une serviette de bain nf | *A bath towel*
Servir v | *To serve*
Ses adj | *His – Her*
Le seuil nm | *The threshold*
Seul – Seule adj | *Alone*
La seule chose adj + nf | *The only thing*
Silencieux – Silencieuse adj | *Silent*
Simple adj | *Simple*
Le soir nm | *The evening*
Le sol nm | *The floor*
Le soleil nm | *The sun*
Le sommeil nm | *Sleep*
Un son nm | *A sound*
Le son nm | *The sound*
Son adj | *His – Her*
Sourd – Sourde adj | *Deaf*
Un sourire nm | *A smile*

Une souris nf | *A mouse*
Sous prep | *Below*
Soutenir v | *To support*
Un souvenir nm | *A souvenir*
Un stylo nm | *A pen*
Su (Savoir) v | *Known (To know)*
Un succès nm | *A success*
Du sucre nm | *Sugar*
Le sud nm | *The South*
Un sujet de conversation nm |
A topic of conversation
Un supermarché nm | *A supermarket*
Sur prep | *On*
Surpris – Surprise adj | *Surprised*
Une surprise nf | *A surprise*
Surveiller v | *To watch*

T

Une table nf | *A table*
Une tache nf | *A spot*
Une tâche nf | *A task*
Du talent nm | *Talent*
Un taille-crayon nm | *A pencil sharpener*
Tailler v | *To prune*
Un talent nm | *A talent*
Un talon nm | *A heel*
Un tapis nm | *A carpet*
Tard adv | *Late*
Une tasse de café nf | *A cup of coffee*
Un taxi nm | *A taxi*
Teindre v | *To dye*
Un téléphone nm | *A phone*
La télévision nf | *The television*
Une tempête nf | *A storm*
Une tempête de neige nf | *A snowstorm*
Le temps nm | *The time*
Le temps nm | *The weather*
Une tente nf | *A tent*
Tes adj | *Your*
Un ticket nm | *A ticket*

Un tiroir nm | *A drawer*
Toi pr | *You*
Un toit nm | *A roof*
Une tomate nf | *A tomato*
Tomber v | *To fall*
Ton adj | *Your*
Une tortue nf | *A turtle*
Tôt adv | *Early*
Toucher v | *To get (for money)*
Toucher v | *To touch*
Toujours adv | *Always*
Un tour nm | *A turn*
Une tour nf | *A tower*
La tour Eiffel nf | *The Eiffel Tower*
Un – Une touriste n | *A tourist*
Tourner v | *To turn*
Tous les matins adv | *Every morning*
Tout adj | *All*
Tout adj | *Everything*
Tout le monde adv | *Everyone else*
Tout le temps | *All the time*
Une traboule nf | *A traboule*
Une trace nf | *A trace*
Un train nm | *A train*
Traiter v | *To treat*
Une tranche de pain nf | *A slice of bread*
Les transports en commun nm |
Public transport
Un travail nm | *A job*
Le travail nm | *Work*
Travailler v | *To work*
Des travaux nm | *Work*
Traverser v | *To run through*
Trier v | *To sort*
Triste adj | *Sad*
Trois n | *Three*
La trouille nf | *Fear*
Une trouvaille nf | *A discovery*
Trouver v | *To find*
Tu pr | *You*
Tu chantes (Chanter) v |
You are singing (To sing)

Tu parles (Parler) v | *I am speaking (To speak)*
Tu t'appelles (S'appeler) v |
You are named (To be named)
Tu veux (Vouloir) v | *You want (To want)*

U

Une université nf | *A college*
Les urgences nf | *The ER/The emergency room*
Utiliser v | *To use*

V

Une valise nf | *A suitcase*
Valoir v | *To be worth*
La vanille nf | *Vanilla*
Vendre v | *To sell*
Un vendeur – Une vendeuse n | *A vendor*
Le vendredi nm | *Friday*
Venir v | *To come*
Le vent nm | *The wind*
Le ventre nm | *The belly*
Vérifier v | *To check*
Un verre nm | *A glass*
Vide adj | *Empty*
Vider v | *To empty*
De la viande nf | *Meat*
La vie de tous les jours nf | *Everyday life*
Une vieille cabane adj + nf | *An old shed*
Une vieille locomotive adj + nf |
An old locomotive
La vieille ville adj + nf | *The old town*
Vieux – Vieille – Vieil adj | *Old*
Un village nm | *A village*
Une ville nf | *A city*
Du vin nm | *Wine*
Du vin blanc nm | *White wine*
Du vin chaud nm | *Mulled wine*
Du vin rouge nm | *Red wine*
Un virus nm | *A virus*

Une visite nf | *A visit*
Visiter v | *To visit*
Un visiteur – Une visiteuse n | *A visitor*
Une visse nf | *A screw*
Vite adv | *Quickly*
Un vitrail nm | *Stained glass*
Vivre v | *To live*
Du vocabulaire nm | *Vocabulary*
Un voisin nm | *A neighbor*
Voir v | *To see*
Une voiture nf | *A car*

Vous pr | *You*
Un voyage nm | *A journey*
Voyager v | *To travel*
Une vraie aventure adj + nf | *A real adventure*
Un vrai plaisir adj + nm | *A real pleasure*
Une vue nf | *A view*

Z

Le zoo nm | *The zoo*

THANK YOU

Thank you for choosing the *French Listening Workbook* as your language-learning companion. I sincerely hope that it helped you improve your French listening skills.

My goal with this book was to provide daily activities that would help you better understand spoken French in all situations. As always, I would greatly appreciate your feedback, so please consider leaving a review where you purchased this workbook.

I always create content for French learners on my YouTube channel, Instagram, or website. You can find all my resources and links at www.theperfectfrench.com.

I hope you find this workbook helpful in your language-learning journey.

Once again, thank you for choosing the *French Listening Workbook*. I wish you all the best in your progress toward becoming more fluent every day!

Dylane

MY BOOKS

The Complete French Courses – Including books, videos, and audio.

> **The Complete French Pronunciation Course**
> **The Complete French Conjugation Course**
> **The Complete French Grammar Course**
> **The Complete French Vocabulary Course**
> **The Complete French Expressions Course**

Conjugation Textbooks – Including books, video, and audio.

> **Passé Composé vs Imparfait**
> **The French Subjunctive**

The French Short Stories – Including books and audio.

> **French Short Stories – Volume 1**
> **French Short Stories – Volume 2**
> **French Long Stories – Volume 3**

My Free Self-Study Guide – Including all my lessons listed and my study plan.

> **The Complete French Self-Study Guide**

Download my free self-study guide at **www.theperfectfrench.com/freebies**.